One-Minute
Mystic

One-Minute Mystic

SIMON PARKE

HAY HOUSE

HAY HOUSE
Australia • Canada • Hong Kong • India
South Africa • United Kingdom • United States

First published and distributed in the United Kingdom by:
Hay House UK Ltd, 292B Kensal Rd, London W10 5BE. Tel.: (44) 20 8962 1230;
Fax: (44) 20 8962 1239. www.hayhouse.co.uk

Published and distributed in the United States of America by:
Hay House, Inc., PO Box 5100, Carlsbad, CA 92018-5100. Tel.: (1) 760 431 7695 or
(800) 654 5126; Fax: (1) 760 431 6948 or (800) 650 5115. www.hayhouse.com

Published and distributed in Australia by:
Hay House Australia Ltd, 18/36 Ralph St, Alexandria NSW 2015.
Tel.: (61) 2 9669 4299; Fax: (61) 2 9669 4144. www.hayhouse.com.au

Published and distributed in the Republic of South Africa by:
Hay House SA (Pty), Ltd, PO Box 990, Witkoppen 2068. Tel./Fax: (27) 11 467 8904.
www.hayhouse.co.za

Published and distributed in India by:
Hay House Publishers India, Muskaan Complex, Plot No.3, B-2, Vasant Kunj, New
Delhi – 110 070. Tel.: (91) 11 4176 1620; Fax: (91) 11 4176 1630. www.hayhouse.co.in

Distributed in Canada by:
Raincoast, 9050 Shaughnessy St, Vancouver, BC V6P 6E5. Tel.: (1) 604 323 7100;
Fax: (1) 604 323 2600

A catalogue record for this book is available from the British Library.

ISBN 978-1-84850-177-5

Pagination by Scribe Design Ltd, Ashford, Kent, UK
Printed and bound in Great Britain by CPI Bookmarque, Croydon CR0 4TD.

All of the papers used in this product are recyclable, and made from wood
grown in managed, sustainable forests and manufactured at mills certified to
ISO 14001 and/or EMAS.

In fond memory of Lewes.

A river passes through it,
and so did we.
So many moments,
and not a moment lost.

A Reading Suggestion

Hop around from chapter to chapter,
like a bumble bee hops from flower to flower.

Don't get stuck in a chapter;
taste briefly, and then taste another,
and then another still.

This is not a linear read,
but a spiral way,
always leaving, always returning.

Here is a random adventure,
pot luck where you open and what you find.

But one flower at a time, and no rush.
Always one flower at a time.

1
Who Am I?

When the Clowning Stops

As the crowd filtered out of the big top and the big band played, Chico the Clown was asked what had been the most frightening part of the evening's performance.

'Well, the stunt where I'm repeatedly knocked over by the swinging plank can have its moments,' he said. 'It's well rehearsed, but much can still go wrong.'

'So that's when you're most fearful?'

'Oh no, not at all!'

'Then when are you most fearful? The unicycle chase? The leap from the elephant? The bucket of custard stunt?'

'None of those, no,' said Chico. 'I'm most fearful after the show, when I get back to the dressing room and take off my colourful coat and big clown's shoes.'

'Why should that be frightening?'

'Ah, because then I must remove my wig and my make-up, look in the mirror and ask myself the same old question: "When the clowning stops, who on Earth are you?"'

Seeing the Glory

'I want to see the glory!' says the seeker.

'Then be still,' says the mystic. 'Stand by the water and you shall see the glory.'

And with that the mystic leaves.

So the seeker stands by the water, but due to recent rain, it is too muddy to see anything. So the seeker, wondering what possible good can come from standing still, wades in, disturbing the water in search of the glory.

And then the mystic returns.

'What are you doing?' they ask. 'I told you to be still. Stay still and you shall see the glory.'

And with that they leave.

So the seeker stands still, but again feels stupid. With the best will in the world, what can this possibly achieve? So again they wade in, disturbing the water in search of the glory.

And then the mystic returns.

'What are you doing?' they ask. 'Didn't I tell you to be still? Stay still and you shall see the glory.'

And with that they leave.

So this time the seeker stays still by the water. And left undisturbed, the muddy water soon becomes clear — clear like a mirror, in which the seeker can see themselves.

'Behold the glory!' says the mystic.

I sometimes feel I achieve more in one minute of staying still than I do in eight hours at work. It's a bit like sitting at the source of a river, where everything begins.

'I'm Like my Dog!'

The man says I will understand him better if I meet his dog.

'I'm just like my dog!' he says.

'Then let me meet your dog,' I reply. 'It would be good to understand you better.'

So he leads me to a yard with high walls where he keeps his dog. He then invites me to step inside, which I do with keen anticipation. As he says, to meet the man I must meet his dog!

Once in the yard, however, I discover not one dog, but hundreds, and no two the same.

'Have you met my dog?' says the man from the other side of the wall, quite unable to see the pack of hounds around me.

'Which one?' I shout back. 'There are so many!'

We are inclined to forget quite how many identities we have. One dog makes the decisions one day, quite another dog the next. We ascribe inconsistency to others but imagine that we ourselves make rational and consistent decisions. Hah!

The good thing about discovering we're a pack of unruly hounds is that we take ourselves less seriously, which, interestingly, frees us to be kind.

The Shape of Things to Come

So, what's tomorrow's forecast?

It's a good question, and I'm not just referring to the weather. Ever since the dawn of history we've been trying to find out what's going to happen next. It's been something we've wanted to know, so that, like the Boy Scouts, we can be prepared.

So we've tried everything: we've done divination with sticks; examined the stars and their signs; listened to prophecy and prediction; turned to tea leaves and the cards; attempted forecasts based on known patterns and statistical probability; sent satellites into space to tell us what they see on the horizon.

I once watched a man in a betting shop follow a fly's progress up the wall. He ended up betting on the horse whose name was in the box where the fly settled. Prophets and forecasters come in all shapes and sizes.

In fact we've left no stone unturned in our attempt to give shape to the future, though to what end, I'm not sure.

I look everywhere for the future, when all the time,
the shape of the future is the shape of my heart.

The Road to Virtue

I am watching the road and this is what I see:

- The cat gives way to the old lady, because she's big and has a stick.
- The old lady gives way to the bicycle, because she's frail and the bicycle's travelling fast.
- The bicycle gives way to the scooter, because the scooter has more power and a protective shield.
- The scooter gives way to the car, because the car is a good deal more solid and could do the scooter serious damage.
- The car gives way to the bus, because it's enormous and the driver looks less than friendly.
- The bus gives way to the giant crane transporter, because the transporter is a monster vehicle – towering and menacing metal.

We do give way to others sometimes, and perhaps think well of ourselves as a result. It can be wise to retreat or adjust occasionally, particularly at work, in the face of someone more powerful. But as I watch the road, it's only when the giant crane transporter gives way to the cat that sweet virtue breaks out.

Until then, it's all just been the dull common sense of self-interest.

The Stupid Woman

I knew a stupid woman once. She couldn't tell you anything important. Take music, for instance. She never knew what a song was called, or who the singer was, or which album it came from. Didn't even know what year it was recorded.

Hopeless! Such a stupid woman. She couldn't tell you anything important about music.

And it was the same with books. She might read a book, but she never knew who'd written it, or what the title was, or who'd published it. (Though she could sometimes tell you what colour the cover was.)

Hopeless! Such a stupid woman.

And whatever you do, don't take her on a field trip. She doesn't know the name of any flower, bird or river.

It makes you wonder where she's been all her life. Hasn't she had any education at all?

Hopeless! Such a stupid woman. She knows nothing. Except...

She does know when music moves her, and when a book speaks to her, and she dances at the impossible beauty of creation.

I wish I was stupid like her.

Salt in our Cup

Most of us are easily upset. It can be the result of a single remark, a look even. Or perhaps it's a nagging worry, the tone of an e-mail or an unexpected event. Whatever it is, our equilibrium is disturbed and our peace destroyed. It's like rain on our parade, like salt in our tea, ruining everything.

Of course, if you put a spoonful of salt in a cup of water, it has horrid power. That's a lot of salt for a small amount of liquid and drinking it may well make you sick. If, however, you put a spoonful of salt in a jug of water, there is less impact. The salt will still be noticed, but not to the same degree, because there's simply more water to absorb it. In the jug, the salt will be struggling to gain your attention.

But here's a thing: if you put a spoonful of salt in a lake, it won't be noticed at all! The lake is way too large. How is a spoonful of salt to have any effect here? In fact, in the lake, it will be exposed for what it is: just a small spoonful of not very much.

Which makes me sense that a mystic is an aspiring lake, forever growing in depth, increasing in capacity and therefore undisturbed by a spoonful here and there.

Acrobatic Decisions

There were once two acrobats who made their living by balancing on a pole. The teacher would hold the pole and the young child would climb it. It wasn't without its dangers, of course. As both audience and acrobats knew, a slip by either of the performers would be a disaster.

Then one day the teacher made a suggestion. He said that if they were to avoid accidents and carry on making their living in this manner, it would be wise if they looked out for each other. He would look out for the child as she climbed and she should look out for him as he held the pole.

But the child had other ideas and said, 'No.'

'No?' said the teacher.

'No,' said the girl. 'I know you are my teacher, but I think it's better that we each watch ourselves. That way I am sure we will avoid accidents and earn enough to make a living.'

I tend to agree with the child. I don't meet many people who will be fit to make decisions about others until they are a good deal wiser about themselves.

The Truth Mirror and the Shop Window

Truth Mirror: You're very brave.

Seeker: Brave? Why d'you call me brave?

TM: Not everyone stands in front of the truth mirror.

S: Why not?

TM: Because I tell the truth about your inner shape.

S: My *inner* shape?!

TM: It's a different kind of seeing – different, say, from taking a glance at yourself reflected in a shop window.

S: Well, I never do that.

TM: There are plenty who do.

S: Not me. Well, just occasionally, maybe. It's possible I did it a long time ago. But only if I was going to a meeting and really had to.

TM: So how you look matters?

S: Of course it matters! If you're going to a party—

TM: Parties as well as meetings?

S: It's important how you present yourself!

TM: And important who you are?

S: Well, maybe. But really, you can't do much about that. The human personality is hard-edged and written in stone.

TM: Or fluid and written in water?

S: Dream on!

TM: Certainly. For my dream is truer than your nightmare…

It's All about the Doormat

Here's a cleaning tip. If we wish to attend to the cleanliness of our house, we'll need to start with the front entrance, where we receive people. If our doormat is filthy, then the rest of the house will be, no matter how hard we scrub elsewhere. Every new arrival will wipe their feet on the filthy mat and then carry the dirt from room to room. Infuriating! And after a while, we'll put our hands in the air in deep frustration. 'How can I possibly keep a clean house? Does it have to be this hard? I feel like giving up!'

It's all about the doormat, the place where people are initially received and welcomed. And likewise in the human psyche, it's the doormat of our first impressions that needs attention. Once we've made that initial negative judgement about someone, for whatever reason – perhaps we've judged their clothes, accent, face or job – our inner space will lack freshness as these negative impressions trample through our home.

If we deal with the doormat of our first impressions, we won't have this trouble.

The Low Point of the Party

When someone is bored with your company at a party, you may find them discreetly looking over your shoulder. They are feeling a little trapped and are wondering if there is someone more interesting or influential on the horizon.

It's rude of them to treat you in this way, and the experience leaves you feeling diminished, uncomfortable and perhaps angry. They have no right to do that! Though, funnily enough, it may be something *you'll* one day do *to yourself.*

There are times when we become bored with ourselves, bored with this character who seems stuck in a rut, doing the same things over and over. We may feel trapped, unhappy with what we are but unable to be anything else. And so we start looking over our own shoulder, bored by ourselves at the party!

It was Rumi who asked why, if the prison door was now open, we insisted on staying inside. It's very hard to leave the familiar. But noticing we are bored with ourselves might be the first sweet step of departure, for life is not a treadmill but an adventure of reinvention and becoming.

Facing the Truth

When I see people in sunglasses for no apparent reason, it reminds me that people wear masks so that they won't be seen. Perhaps we fear there's nothing within us to see. Or perhaps we know there's plenty to be seen, none of which we like very much, and so we wear a mask. It might be a false face of hilarity, or of fashion, competence, indifference, superiority, goodness, insouciance or victimhood – whatever gets us through. We may have more than one mask, depending on our setting.

Masks are effective at covering us up and can fool most of the people most of the time. But there are problems. When we are wearing a mask we can't feel the sun on our face for a start, which is very sad. The sun is there to warm us, but masks deny us its golden touch. Neither can we feel the breeze on our face, which again is sad, because it's cooling and puts us in gentle contact with our surroundings.

And in the end, a mask is a solution to nothing, fatally separating us from others. People wear masks so they will not be seen, when what they want most of all is the precise opposite: they long to be seen!

All Hands on Deck

The ship made its way through the water in slightly troubled fashion, never quite settling on a direction. It was a strange sight to behold. But with no captain, what else would you expect?

Apparently the deckhands were taking it in turns to steer, with no member of the crew holding the wheel for long. One of them took the ship in one direction before being pushed away by another, who changed course completely! And such changes happened many times in the day.

And I tell the story now, for I am that ship. I may like to imagine a sensible captain is standing at my wheel, a constant on the voyage. The reality, however, is different. For I am many people, each one grabbing at the wheel and strutting his stuff before disappearing into the crowd.

It's a concern in a way, though in acknowledging my chaos I perhaps become less dangerous to those around me. As the ship of my psyche struggles through the seas, I shall not claim an unchanging and consistent core at my centre –

and neither shall I expect it in others.

Teaching the Duckling New Things

When is a good teacher a terrible thing? When they teach you unhappiness. And unhappiness *is* taught, rather than being a natural part of our lives.

When we were children, we learned well from our teachers. We imbibed everything, too small to realize the dull poison our soft skin absorbed.

And though we've grown up now and left many childish ways behind, this way we've retained, the way of unhappiness. And who can blame us? We had good teachers and it's the only path we know.

They do say that a duckling follows the first thing it sees when born. If it were to see a fox, would it perhaps follow that? Until it was eaten.

Learning to be happy is a wise move, and allowed.

Entirely Different?

In his brilliant new book the author savagely debunks all that has gone before, and the critics love it. 'Ground-breaking stuff!' declares the excited reviewer. 'It's so different!'

And see the charismatic politician rising to popularity and power as a new broom. 'This country needs change!' he declares to the adoring cameras, while his spin doctor tells us, 'He's so different!'

And then in the Gospel stories, see the Pharisees standing proud in the market place, robed and holy, thanking God they are not like other people. 'There are some bad sorts out there,' they say. 'But thank God we're different!'

And, like them, we can look around us and acquire the deadening habit of defining ourselves against other people. Whether in the manner of the debunking author or the new-broom politician or the stand-apart Pharisees, we begin to imagine it's important that we are not as others are. In fact, let's be honest, our insecure ego will do almost anything to appear different.

And why? Because somewhere deep inside, it suspects it's just the same as everyone else, and though it can cope with many things, it really can't cope with that.

The Outhouse

A river ran by it, the crumbling stone outhouse in the chateau garden. And I was to clear it out, after years of neglect.

A surprised water rat scuttled away as I entered, for no one had been there for years. And in the half-light afforded by boarded windows, it was hard at first to see what was useful and what wasn't. Here junk merged with jewel, trash with treasure. So my first move was to clear the space. I took everything outside, laid it on the grass and contemplated it all in the warm light of the summer's day.

I then lit a bonfire, because much here had served its time – useful once, but no longer so, and best given to the flames.

But the sunlight also revealed much that was good. There was a solid table, for instance, which just needed a clean; a large amount of string, which required only some unravelling; and bamboo sticks that could still support tomatoes. There was also a beautiful old portrait which I cleaned up and took inside the chateau, where it now hangs.

I don't know how long it had been there or who it was, but it felt like a morning spent looking at my life and finding myself.

Leaving Home

The woman asked me how she should live her life from that time on. She said she had no more solutions, she'd tried them all.

I said that without knowing her particular situation, I could only say certain things.

'What things?' she asked.

I said that if she was serious, she should prepare for a journey. I suggested she travel light – perhaps just pack sandwiches and a drink – and then leave by the front door.

'Close the gate behind you and walk for a while. It doesn't matter where you walk, because it's not the direction that matters.

'Voices will soon start telling you to turn back, but ignore them, for you were right to set out and are right now to continue. So carry on walking, for it's the walking that matters, and when you're tired, the voices will return, telling you to build a house, like the one you've left behind. Ignore these voices as well, for you were right to leave the house you inhabited; it was a house of unhappiness.

'Instead, inhabit yourself and allow your body to love what it loves. Having tried to save everyone, it's now time to save yourself.

'And after rest and refreshment, journey on, half-knowing but wholehearted, allowing new scenes and new ways to look after you.

'And it's not about direction. Just aim for the horizon and notice everything.'

Old Ghosts

Sometimes I declare myself to be worried. 'I am so worried!' I say, and believe this to be so. My worry is the most obvious thing in the world. And haven't I every reason to be worried?

Like a dark cloud across the sun, a worry clouds my psyche and I begin to hallucinate, imagining the worry to be me. Yes, I seem somehow defined by it. I move from noticing a concern passing through to the sense that this is who I am: I *am* this worry!

I am *not* this worry, of course. Like most distressing emotions, it is a distant memory acting up, a childish panic resurrected. My present circumstances jangle old bells and stir old ghosts, but a worry wort? Not me!

I am peace, that is who I am, while old ghosts trespass on land that isn't theirs.

The Mighty River and the Small Hill

This is the story of a very mighty river and a pathetically small hill. And in the story, the mighty river flows up to the small hill and demands that it give way, so that it might continue on, sweeping majestically through the countryside, which is what it likes to do.

'Give way this instant!' says the mighty river to the hill. 'I am a mighty river and you, as a pathetically small hill, must give way to me!'

The hill, which has been there a while, is puzzled. It can hear a small voice, but however hard it looks, it can see no mighty river.

'Where are you?' asks the hill.

'I'm here!' says the little voice. 'And I'm a mighty river! No question about it! So give way, I say!'

Finally, after much squinting, the hill locates the source of the voice: in a field nearby, there is a water droplet on a donkey's ear.

Our ego can get carried away with its own imaginings and bring unhappiness all round. Seeing life only through the lens of our needs and desires makes us the directors of our very own nightmare.

An Invented Story

There are many great and wonderful inventions in the world, but this isn't one of them, it really isn't. And the invention in question is *me*, for, yes, much of me is invented. Much was dreamed up and cobbled together when I was young and thought mainly of survival. My panic, anxiety and fear – indeed, all the emotions that bring suffering to my day, like guilt and negativity – these are the most unfortunate of inventions, not worthy of any drawing board and certainly nothing to do with who I am.

The real me does not suffer daily but enjoys the adventurous unfolding of life around me and through me, like a fountain in a dry place. It is my invented self who suffers – full of dodgy parts, held together by inexpert welding, hopelessly compromised by cranky perceptions and the need for particular outcomes.

'Did you have a good day?' someone asks me.

I think back to my countless reactions and jerky changes of mood and reply, 'Oh, so-so. Up and down, you know.'

But this isn't true. I had a great day, a really excellent one. It was just my invented self who struggled.

2
Observe
Yourself

Reduced Circumstances

We live in reduced circumstances, like a lord and lady thrown out of their castle and confined to a small dark caravan.

The human brain is a very efficient filter, sifting out any information not relevant to our survival. If something cannot be reduced to a shape that makes us feel secure or better about ourselves, the brain simply edits it out of our awareness.

If this deadening filter is removed, of course, things look very different. Our reduced circumstances expand considerably and we see as Adam and Eve saw on that first day of creation – every common thing aglow with inner wonder. As William Blake said, 'If the doors of perception were cleansed, everything would appear to man as it is – infinite.'

Oh, and some good news just in. Remember the lord and lady thrown out of their castle and confined to a small dark caravan?

Well, apparently they've just opened the curtains and discovered a remarkable view!

The Guru's Word

The crowd thought the guru was the bee's knees in the spirituality world – certainly in the top five, anyway – and so they pressed him again and again for a special word.

'Give us a word to change the world!' they said, because they really wanted to change the world and had bookcases to prove it.

The guru raised his eyebrows a little wearily, because he wanted to sit with the moon and felt words were overrated. But the crowd would not take no for an answer and pressed some more.

'Then at least give us a word to change ourselves!' they said, because they really wanted to change themselves and had bookcases to prove it.

The guru smiled and, with his finger, wrote a word in the sand.

'At last!' they all thought, eagerly gathering round to read the guru's word.

After which they grumbled, cursed him and then beat him up.

'What a joke!' said one. 'Charlatan!' declared another. 'Just another phoney!' added a third.

Then, consumed with frustration, they messed up the sand and destroyed his stupid word: 'Notice.'

Everyone wants to change the world; no one wants to notice themselves.

Of Mice and Men and Women

'Agghh!'

When I first see a mouse in the kitchen, it's the worst thing, because they frighten me.

And then, as I recover from the initial shock, I reassure myself: 'Perhaps there's just the one?'

But I know this isn't true. I've been told that by the time you see one mouse, there are many others well settled, probably in the back of the sofa.

So then I think, 'Oh, I wish I hadn't seen it tonight. It's going to ruin the whole evening!'

A short while later, however, after a few ruined moments, the first bit of good news filters into my awareness: 'Well, at least I can do something about it now. With infestations, ignorance is only bliss for so long.'

And actually, that's not just true for mice.

'That's What I Want'

Everyone knows what they want, or rather, they think they do. A friend of mine wanted to leave London for 20 years to live in the country. She got her dream in the end, got away from it all. But she was back in London two years later, disillusioned. 'It wasn't what I wanted after all,' she said. 'And what worries me is this: I felt so sure.'

Long ago, the Persian poet Rumi invited us to be suspicious about what we want. 'I ride after a deer,' he says, 'and find myself chased by a hog. I dig pits to trap others — and fall in them myself!'

We desire things, chase after them, but often discover more sawdust than glitter.

There will always be trial and error in these things. After all, how can we know what we want until it is given to us and then tested? We may speculate about the peach in the greengrocer's, but until it's in our mouth, we really can't know what it's like. Only then are we able to say, 'Yes, this is good,' or, 'No, this is not what I imagined.'

It's not *wanting* that is unhelpful, but *worship* of the want, as though it is a self-evident truth: 'Only this will make me happy! I know it will!'

Like walking across an icy pond, we must trust a little to proceed, but without putting all our weight anywhere.

Removing your Head

Without wishing to alarm you, it is probably best if you cut off your head today, or at least ignore it, for it seriously distracts you from happiness.

In essence, you are like a delighted child: pure, curious and happy. Like a mountain stream, this young and open spirit bubbles in our bodies with life and wonder and is extremely good company.

Yet daily, we say goodbye to all that; daily we exchange wonder for worry, as we become entangled in the thoughts and schemes of our head, which is a persuasive and many-tentacled mental monster. We identify with our thoughts. A sense of 'I' and 'me' creeps into our dealings with people, a primitive pride, a sense of entitlement, claim or offence. 'They don't like my thoughts and schemes – how dare they?!' Or, 'This had better work out as I planned or I'll be furious!' And suddenly happiness is a long way away.

Which is why it is best if we cut off our heads and identify instead with our delighted child. Then, with a chuckle, we can let go of the restless crowd of our many thoughts. They are passing through, of no fixed abode, moving on – the meaningless shouts of drunks late on a Saturday night…

Good Days, Bad Days

There have been many good days in the history of the human race. There was the discovery of fire, for instance, which made so many new recipes possible; the invention of the wheel, which revolutionized the transport of dead mammoths and package holidays to Stonehenge; and the first fresh loaf of bread, with an aroma that stilled even the fiercest of Neanderthal rows. Those were good days.

But a really bad day was when someone first put their hands on their hips in disapproval and said: 'Well, I'm afraid you'll just have to wait.' That day was a complete disaster, for the idea spread like ground elder. Suddenly, everyone started waiting for something in the future. 'We'll just have to wait!' they said. 'There's something good ahead, but we'll just have to wait!' Some waited for this, others waited for that and some even waited for the other. But all without exception ran madly from the one place where life can be found – and that's the present moment.

Planning future happiness is like writing in water.

Mixed Messages

She was quite baffled as she pulled people towards her and then pushed them away. Why did they react so disappointingly towards her?

'Come to me, go away from me, come to me, go away from me.'

That was what she said to everyone. Where was the problem?

'Come to me, go away from me, come to me, go away from me.'

The message was clear enough, surely?

Yet sometimes people acted so strangely towards her, as if it wasn't clear what she wanted, which was all very painful.

'Come to me, go away from me, come to me, go away from me.'

How could she be any clearer than that?

The Good Guru Guide

When a guru knocks on your door, declaring themselves to be the answer to life, the universe and everything, pause a moment in a quiet place and before signing up:

1. Beware the one who imagines their spiritual experience must be imposed on everyone else; that their particular discovery can be generalized as truth for everyone.

2. Beware the paranoid guru who declares that you are either 'in' or 'out' and denounces those who are out as stupid, lost or infidels.

3. Beware of slick or persuasive oratory that somehow draws you in; for oratory is a key tool of manipulation.

4. Beware the guru who attracts disciples but not friends; who considers themselves above others in some way.

5. Beware the guru who is more interested in their ideas (and little empire of DVDs, conferences and books) than in people.

6. Beware the guru who needs followers to bolster their own ego; for whom a hundred phoney conversations beat one real one.

7. Beware the guru who promises way too much.

8. *But – and it's a big but – welcome the guru who gives you back to yourself in joyful delight, because it is your journey and not theirs.*

Boxed and Sorted

Everyone has spiritual experiences, because everyone is spiritual. But have you noticed what happens then? Some people take their spiritual experiences and make a religion out of them.

This is understandable. Turning something into a religion, with its own creeds and commands, helps to formalize the experience, tidies things up a bit. It's like gathering up our scattered toys and putting them in a box so we can show Aunty. It brings order to things.

But then a change of language can be discerned. Instead of saying, 'Here are my experiences,' we say, 'Here is my religion.' All boxed and sorted!

Boxes are useful for brief storage. Where would we be without them? But in the long term, they can get airless and the things inside them stale.

This is why mystics sometimes struggle with organized religion.

You'll know what's best for you.

And fair's fair — religions have produced some of the greatest mystics of all time.

The Colour of Grass

On Monday, the man told me that grass was often green. I said, 'How ridiculous!' and argued my case rather well. I wasn't letting him get away with that!

On Tuesday, the man told me that grass was often green. I said I'd occasionally seen green grass, but not to the extent he suggested. No way! There are always people like him, trying it on.

On Wednesday, the man told me that grass was often green. I can't remember exactly how I replied, though I trust I was open to his point of view. I had no wish to be impolite and he had a right to his opinion.

On Thursday, the man told me that grass was often green. It was good to see him again and anyone could see his words had a ring of truth. Grass being green is hardly controversial!

On Friday, I told the boy that grass was often green. He said, 'How ridiculous!' and argued vehemently against my position with barely concealed disdain.

We can only receive what we are ready to receive and understand what we are ready to understand. Until then, there isn't a force in the world, nuclear or otherwise, that can break through our defences.

Beware the Horizon

Is being a seeker one of the least spiritual things we can do? Quite possibly.

One of the problems with seeking is that we may well find what we seek, but become blind to everything else. We see what we want on the horizon, but in rushing towards it become oblivious to everything else around us.

'Ah! There is the answer!' we shout in delight. 'At last! Nothing else now matters! Out of my way, everyone!'

With clear goals before them, seekers may achieve their objective in an organized sort of way. But how much do they discover? True discovery is having no goals, no objectives, just feeling free, open and rushing madly towards nothing –

because you are already there.

Why the Mystic Was Late

This short piece explains why the mystic was late for the Grand Garden Opening.

The re-landscaping of the gardens had been brilliant, if expensive; there was even a film star to open them. But the mystic was late.

They weren't held up in traffic; in fact, they got off the bus near the entrance with at least 15 minutes to spare. And the neon signs could not have been clearer: 'Grand Garden Opening this way!' All the mystic had to do was follow the large crowd moving as one towards the entrance.

But the mystic was late because on leaving the bus, they couldn't help but notice a dandelion growing beneath the pavement hedge. It was a wonderful flower, though no one else seemed aware of it.

'Don't you just love nature?!' the crowd said, rushing lemming-like past the fragile yellow glory. 'Apparently, the whole thing's cost over a million pounds! And that doesn't include the Hollywood hunk!'

The mystic, however, stayed for some time in happy wonder with the dandelion, arrived late for the Grand Opening and missed the film star completely.

Which reminds me, they do say the most beautiful flower in the world grew in a forest and was seen by no one.

The Impossible Question

'So here's a question for you,' says the strange man.

'Ask away!' you answer.

'It's a "just suppose" question.'

'That's OK.'

'You have to imagine a situation.'

'I know what to do!'

'Just suppose you had to choose between your favourite guru and the truth. Which would you choose?'

'I can't answer that because it would never happen.'

'I know, I know. But just suppose it did and you had to jump one way or the other – which way would you jump?'

'It's an impossible question. Ask me another one.'

'I'm asking you this one.'

'But my guru always speaks the truth.'

'Of course, of course. But humour me in my madness. And just suppose that you had to choose between your messiah and the truth – which would you choose?'

You lower your voice and check the door is closed.

'I'd choose the truth,' you say.

'Ah! Then one day you might be a mystic!' says the man, though he could have been an angel.

Draw your own Conclusions

Here's a story that goes in one direction and then another, and all as true as toast.

The girl in the store was distraught when her friend was murdered. Who wouldn't be? A street killing after an argument – where's the sense in that?

'Whoever did it, they should lock him up and throw away the key!' she said with venom.

Only then she discovered she knew the murderer. In fact, she knew him better than the boy who had been killed. The victim had been a school friend, but the murderer she'd known since nursery – a more binding allegiance.

'How could they give him such a long sentence?!' she wailed.

Which all goes to remind me never to trust my conclusions – they will tend to be more personal than truthful.

'Kindly Proceed'

How we perceive is how we proceed; this is how it is.

As the ancient saying goes: to the lover, the beautiful woman is perceived as a delight; to the monk, she is a distraction; and to the mosquito, she is lunch. So they proceed differently: the lover runs longingly towards her, the monk deliberately looks away and the mosquito settles on her arm and takes a large bite.

How we perceive is how we proceed; we perceive things to be a certain way and make judgements and decisions on that basis.

And so it was that just the other day I felt the need to forgive someone for a perceived slight. I was surprised by the result. As I forgave them, I felt a change in my body and a gentle loosening of my facial muscles. I was free and so were they!

However, I later discovered that my oh-so-noble act of forgiveness was entirely misplaced, as my perceptions turned out to be wrong – really quite wide of the mark. There was nothing to forgive. And so my inward direction changed: I now forgave myself for my ridiculous perceptions and reminded myself to be more wary of them in future.

Better trust a mouse with the cheese than trust our perceptions.

Out Shopping on a Windless Day

I was out shopping, needing some milk, when I passed a woman in the street. She was walking in the opposite direction to me and complaining about the wind. Well, I had to smile, for it was a windless day! Really, I could feel no wind at all.

'Here is a woman with a vigorous imagination,' I thought, and pitied her for not having my firm grasp of reality.

Perhaps my smile betrayed my thoughts, for then she spoke.

'If you can't feel the wind, sir, it's probably behind you.'

'Ridiculous!' I thought and hurried on.

Though on my return journey I may have complained a little about the wind in my face.

The Angry Puppet

You enter a room and the familiar puppet greets you.

'Hello!' it says. 'Me again!'

'Hello,' you say wearily.

'Same as usual?' asks the puppet.

'No,' you say, because to be honest, you're a bit bored with the usual.

'*No?*' screams the puppet. '*No?* What do you mean, "No"?!'

'The usual isn't getting me anywhere,' you say.

'Well, where do you want to get to?'

'I don't know.'

'There's nowhere to go anyway! Trust me.'

And then you say something rather startling: 'Can I please speak to the puppeteer?'

'I beg your pardon!' says the puppet.

'I don't want to speak to the puppet any more, I want to speak to the puppeteer.'

'I don't know what you mean!' says the angry puppet. 'What puppeteer? You're talking nonsense!'

Sometimes it is good to speak not to your phoney self but to your true self – the one beneath the layers of personality that formed during your early years; the one that perhaps is different from the self you present to the world.

The puppet will be furious, of course; absolutely livid. It imagines itself the decision maker, the great 'I am'. But it's more like the Great Pretender, to be honest. And you are worth more than that – worth an audience with your true self, the puppeteer.

The Wisdom of Boxing

I was listening to a boxing man, a trainer of boxers. He ran a gym and offered his aspiring fighters some basic rules if they wanted to make it in this most dangerous of games. This is what he said:

Rule no. 1: Stay humble – the day you think you're something special, you're over.

Rule no. 2: Keep working – you only get as much as you put in.

Rule no. 3: Don't disrespect your opponent; never think you have them understood and in your pocket.

Rule no. 4: Don't imagine you can tell what someone will do just by the way they look.

I listened in awe – such wonderful rules, and yes, to be lived daily. I just wanted to add one more:

Rule no. 5: *There are no opponents.*

The Search

They had looked everywhere, they really had. They'd scoured the streets and walked the hills outside town. They'd checked car parks, schools and shops.

They'd turned their homes upside down, flown over the desert and surveyed the sea. They'd looked in the office filing cabinets and behind the sofa cushions at home where things usually were.

They'd gone back to the bus stop, returned to the playground and taken a torch down the mines. North, south, east and west they'd looked! Up in the sky, on the dark side of the moon, in the stars and behind the bushes near the bike sheds.

They'd looked everywhere, left no stone unturned. But, exhausted, they finally gave up. They just had to accept they hadn't found it.

Not that any of them knew what they were looking for. And that can make the search a lot harder.

An Absolute Waste of Time

So what's an absolute waste of time? That's right – telling a bald man hair-raising stories.

But if, having done that, you have more time to waste, why not spend the rest of the day inwardly justifying the way you behave and judging others accordingly? This also is an absolute waste of time.

Here's what happens: from your moral high ground, your impression of someone becomes an opinion, your opinion becomes a judgement, and your judgement brings death, thereby both solving nothing and creating nothing. It's futility in a nutshell.

No, really, just imagine it! Solving nothing! And creating nothing! Apart from hell of course.

And I hear there's been an over-order in that department already...

The Chemistry Set

'I wanted to buy you a chemistry set, Melvin.'

'Well, thank you, Aunty, but—'

'I looked at it and thought, "That's for Melvin!" I just knew!'

'It's kind, but—'

'I was fascinated by it, really gripped – took me back to my own childhood, you see!'

'That's nice for you, Aunty.'

'I used to love my chemistry set – all the little bits and bobs, the different-coloured chemicals, the distinctive aromas!'

'Really?'

'Oh, yes. It was given to me by my Uncle Jim. Always my favourite uncle, of course – always gave me the best presents!'

'But I hate chemistry.'

'And you'll also like this, Melvin. It's a book about the history of chemistry. I stood in the shop for hours reading it!'

Your great acts of love – who are they for, exactly?

A Terrible Revenge

'I have the answer!' exclaimed Duped, the sick genius intent on revenge against the human race. 'I know how to bring endless unhappiness and slavery, how to turn them into machines even!'

'So what's the plan?' asked Side Kick, his untrusted lackey.

'The celebrity culture! Through education and the media, I will make everyone wish to be like someone else, someone famous or with money. "I must *be* someone!" they will say. They will have goals and objectives!'

'But aren't those quite a good thing?' asked Side Kick.

'A good thing? They're a complete nightmare! They'll bring an endless cycle of disappointment and envy! The moment someone wants something, they're no longer free!'

'I hadn't thought of that,' said Side Kick, moderately impressed by his master's reasoning.

'They will fear all things – fear not being, fear not acquiring, fear not arriving! They will be little more than machines of fear, and my revenge will be complete. Wonderful!'

Side Kick applauded outwardly, but privately he reckoned no one would be so stupid as to exchange present beauty and peace for all that nonsense.

Punishing Times

Two young men stood at the bar and talked about their childhoods. In particular, they discussed how they had been punished when young.

'Did your dad cane you?' asked the taller of the two.

'Never,' said the other. 'He had this great big book on child psychology.'

'Must have been great!'

'No – he used to hit me with that instead.'

Tend your heart, not your bookshelf.

3

The Valley
of Decision

The Gold Curtains

The house was squalid inside. So when the owner was offered some fine gold curtains to put in his window, he leapt at the chance. People would see them and declare his house a fine house. 'Have you seen the wonderful gold curtains?' they would say. 'How the house has changed!'

But though the curtains hung beautifully in the window, the house remained damp and dirty inside and quite overrun by vermin. The householder made no changes inside, thinking his new curtains on public show would do the trick.

This was a shame, for because the house didn't change, the curtains did. Dust settled, layer by layer, dimming the shine; the damp rotted the fabric and the vermin ran up and down, snagging the fine golden thread with their claws. It was not long before the once fine curtains were reduced to the level of the rest of the house and became a cause of resentment to the householder.

'I had such high hopes of them!' he said sniffily. 'But they are most disappointing.'

Truth is not separate from its setting; it grows within us or rots revoltingly.

Shedding Skins

Have you ever watched a snake shed its skin? When the time comes, it isn't at all sentimental – it just leaves it in the grass and moves on. It does this when it no longer needs it, when the old skin has served its purpose and the new skin is ready – ready for fresh adventures.

The snake sheds the old skin because it is wrinkled, dry and uncomfortable and has no more life in it.

Are you as wise as the snake? What are you like with old skins? Do you cling or let go? You've probably played many roles down the years, and not all of them by choice – sometimes circumstances dictate. Maybe you are prouder of some roles than others, but that's all right. As someone once said, 'To live is to change, and to be perfect is to have changed often.'

And if you were a snake, counting your old skins today, how many would there be? If you had time, you could even move through the grass, visiting old sites and roles now abandoned. Which have happy memories and which make you sad or angry?

Some people cling on to their old wrinkled skins, because they cannot believe there's fresh skin beneath. 'I know what I like, and I like what I know!' they say. No offence, but that's as sensible as hoarding mouldy bread in case it comes in handy one day.

Bus-Stop Dilemmas

The question is, how long do you stand at the bus stop?

You've been here a while now, standing in the rain, gazing hopefully down the road. The first few minutes were all right – you used the time to make a phone call – but it's been a while now. You've watched the corner intently, willing the bus to appear. You've even thought you heard it, only for a lorry to swing into view. That false dawn made you even more impatient.

So how long do you stand at the bus stop? How long do you wait to be picked up? The fact is, you've got a lot to do and need to be getting on, which makes this delay frustrating. Surely the bus must come soon? I mean, why offer a bus service if it doesn't deliver when you most need it?

So how long do you stand at the bus stop? How long before you decide that you're going to walk? How long before you decide that waiting for others to do something for you is not always the best idea?

And so you start to walk, and find it surprisingly enjoyable. Even the sky seems to clear in celebration of your courage. And you're fit and strong! You hadn't quite realized it during all those years of waiting for a bus.

Waiting for another to come along and save you…

'Doctor, Doctor'

A man walks confidently into a doctor's surgery and sits down.

'What seems to be the problem?' asks the doctor.

'I want to be treated for my broken leg,' says the patient.

'Really?' says the doctor, looking at the man's two healthy legs, but noticing a gash on his head.

'Yes, I want to be treated for my leg.'

'I see,' says the doctor. 'Perhaps you could first jog on the spot for 30 seconds?'

The man does so with some ease and then sits down again.

'You're sure you wish to be treated for a broken leg?' asks the doctor.

'Definitely!'

'But your leg isn't broken.'

'Not broken? What do you mean? It's why I'm here!'

'Mmm,' says the doctor thoughtfully, as blood rushes from the man's head wound. 'How about I treat what's really wrong with you?'

The patient looks surprised and thinks for a while, then finally agrees.

'Yes, I'm all for that,' he says with a smile.

'Grand!' says the doctor. 'I'll treat what's really wrong with you.'

'I'm happy with that!' says the patient. 'Just so long as what's really wrong with me is a broken leg.'

Please don't lose any more blood through hallucination.

Offensive Behaviour

You have been told there is nothing to bring to the party. 'Bring yourself and nothing else!' That is what the invitation said.

But you can hardly bring nothing! That just wouldn't be right.

So when the day comes, you turn up with a bottle of wine and some home-made sandwiches, which you proudly give to the host.

'Thank you,' he says with a smile, 'but I don't want them.'

'I'm sure they'll come in useful,' you say.

'No, they won't, they really won't. There's plenty here. That's why I said not to bring anything.'

'Oh, I always bring something!' you say. 'I like to pay my way.'

'There's no need.'

'But I insist!'

The host then takes the sandwiches and throws them in the bin, after which he goes outside and smashes the bottle of wine against the wall, tossing the broken glass into a skip. He then turns back towards you.

'Welcome!' he says cheerfully. 'Come on in!'

Welcome? Come on in? How can he say that, after what he's just done?

Don't bring your strengths to the task of being a mystic. They're not needed and may get binned or smashed.

The Truth Mirror and the Only Thing to Fear

Truth Mirror: Nothing I say will harm you.

Seeker: That sounds ominous.

TM: I'll go further: everything I say will help you.

S: That sounds even more ominous. Coating a bitter pill with chocolate? I've tried it with my dog – it doesn't work.

TM: Why imagine truth is bitter?

S: It threatens my illusions and I need them!

TM: Your illusions need you, but you don't need them. You're better than that.

S: Flattery will get you everywhere.

TM: It's not flattery, just plain psychological fact. Take the person who feels frightened inside and so creates a tough outer persona that people find unpleasant.

S: I know someone like that.

TM: Instead of facing the problem, their fear, they create an illusion: 'I'm tough!' It's all nonsense, of course, and loses them friends. But worse, it stops them discovering the truth that there's nothing to be frightened of anyway!

S: I suppose so.

TM: All truth is a friend, sweet and not bitter. So fear nothing.

S: *Nothing?*

TM: Nothing except that which cuts you off from the truth…

A Disappointed Fan

'Tell me about mysticism!'

'Why?'

'It sounds exciting.'

'Oh.'

'I'm weary of people and weary of work. I require higher and more spiritual things!'

'Then go away.'

'Go away?! I've only just arrived!'

'Go away.'

'That is so rude, and me one of your biggest fans!'

'Come back when you're weary of higher and more spiritual things and require work and people.'

What Will You Do?

Good news. I have three very important things to tell you.

Take it from me, they are words you can rely on. Three pearls of wisdom, hewn clean and sharp from the rock of understanding. You will be much the better for hearing them.

These are three very important truths, so no more prevarication or delay! You'll be eager for them, so here goes!

Only I've forgotten what they are.

The three important things…

Nope. They've gone. I can't remember any of them.

This happens sometimes, if I don't write things down.

What will you do without self-important people like me telling you how to live your life?

The Leap

You find me watching a figure standing at the edge of a chasm.

I think they're wondering whether to attempt the leap across.

It's not an impossible leap, but neither is it an easy decision.

It seems they don't wish to turn back; that whatever they have left behind they have left behind for good.

But then again, they are risking a lot by leaping forward. You can never be sure of the strength in your legs and the drop below is a cold and yawning deep.

As I watch, I'm not sure which course of action they'll choose.

Perhaps the moment of conversion comes when the chasm between our actual selves and our desired selves is just so wide that we can no longer ignore it. And then we must leap — for what have we to lose?

Not That Smart

We are told to be SMART with our goals.

Or at least that's what the counsellor said to me:

'Specific, measurable, achievable, realistic and time-based = SMART! Get the idea?'

I got the idea, but remained uncomfortable.

'What about the wild horses within?' I asked.

'Wild horses? What wild horses?!' The counsellor couldn't hide their mirth.

'The wild horses of personality that drag me this way and that and throw me around?'

But the counsellor was seeing another client by the time I finished the sentence.

On reflection, if someone came to me wanting change, I'd recommend TRUTH above SMART:

To remain unattached to horses.

Pond Life

The pond had once been a place of great beauty, a place where ducks swam, water flowed and people naturally gathered. Who wouldn't want to spend an hour or two there when the sun was out? Indeed, it was such an attractive spot that soon tea shops and a boat-hire business appeared, with vending machines for drinks and sweets.

Seeing the beauty, the local council put on their planning hats. In order to preserve things, they decided to build a duck sanctuary, using concrete ledges, oh, and they cleverly closed the water channels in and out of the pond to stop any loss of water – you never quite knew what would happen if you left nature to itself!

No one can be sure of the exact moment when the beautiful pond became a stagnant pool of oil and litter or when the overfed ducks left their bread for the scrambling rats.

No doubt much of your beauty, too, was destroyed with the best of intentions.

The Garden of Sadness

If you come across the Garden of Sadness, don't rush by too quickly.

People tend to avoid it by some means or other. They see the sign up ahead and suddenly invent an important appointment or remember something they must do immediately. Some even jump on the first bus to come round the corner, not bothered as to where it's going as long as it takes them away from the garden! Anywhere but there! They say to themselves, 'Oh, life's too short for all that nonsense!' or 'That's not a can of worms I wish to open' or 'Onwards and upwards!'

But the Garden of Sadness is on everyone's route home and by avoiding it people can lose their way.

Were they to visit the garden, they might be pleasantly surprised through their tears; surprised that weeping for things lost or denied waters the soil of the heart, so that hope and kindness can grow.

We will all pass through this garden's strange beauty on our way home.

Mad Adventures in Silence

So, in the end, I decide to have a go. Many have tried and failed, many think it's a ridiculous thing to do. And in a way, I agree with them.

But nothing ventured, nothing gained. So I put down my magazine and turn off both radio and telly. I turn off my mobile and sit down alone.

I feel restless and decide this is a waste of time. I glance at the magazine cover, but look away. What am I doing here?

In the early silence, a thousand thoughts spring to mind, two thousand anxieties and half a dozen half-baked schemes.

Though I do notice my breathing for the first time today, which is reassuring; it keeps me alive apparently. And it steadies and settles as I sit in growing awareness of the small universe that is me.

When I first sat down, it was the silence that was unreal, but now, as the minutes pass, it's the noise that feels a fraud, the mental noise I insist on most of the time. I'm like a storm-tossed sea becoming calm.

Sure, it's mad what I'm doing, sitting here listening to each breath.

But if I can't be alone with myself, then am I fit to be with anyone else?

An Easy Life

If you want an easy life, choose something simple and undemanding:

- Swim the English Channel to France and back in mid-January.
- Navigate a yacht round the world blindfold.
- Take a log raft down the Amazon with no crocodile repellent on board.
- Run a daily marathon.
- Raise the *Titanic*, solo.
- Climb Everest with just a woolly jumper for the cold.
- Traverse the Arctic Circle in flip-flops.
- Jog across the Sahara with weights.

As I say, if you want an easy life, choose something simple and relatively undemanding.

But if you fancy a challenge, try this: flee partiality and labels and acquire the mystic's single commitment: union with reality, oneness with all that is.

'How Will I Know?'

'But how will I know when I get there?'

'Oh, you'll know, you'll know.'

'Will there be large neon signs warning me?'

'Not as such, no.'

'Will the weather be different?'

'No.'

'Will it be hotter – you know, with all the flames?'

'No.'

'So tell me, just how will I know that I've reached the doorstep of hell?'

'You really want to know?'

'Of course!'

'When you consider people, events and situations solely in terms of how they affect you, that is the doorstep of hell.'

The Child and the Clown

As the crowd filtered out of the big top and the big band played, the child was asked what they had most enjoyed about the circus.

'I liked it all!' they said, inching forward in the hotdog queue.

'And what do you remember the most?'

'Well,' said the child, pausing a moment. 'I liked the people on the high wire, because it was a bit scary, and I also liked the horses, because they looked so beautiful. But I liked the clown best of all.'

'And why did you like the clown?'

'I don't know, really.'

'There must be a reason.'

'Because they made me feel happy sad.'

'Can you explain what you mean?'

'They made me feel sad happy.'

The Terrible Tiger Story

After much discussion, they decided to go ahead and have a tiger as a family pet.

The great day arrived and the tiger was delivered. But it was so frightening they immediately had to act. If the tiger was to stay, certain changes had to be made. First of all, it would need to be kept sedated at all times – the animal had way too much energy! They also had its most dangerous teeth removed, as those fangs could do untold damage; you had to be aware of health and safety. They then put blinkers on its eyes, to make it less aware of its surroundings. And of course they shaved its magnificent fur daily; hoping that ultimately it would forget it was a tiger.

If it gave up on being a tiger, it would be much easier for all of them.

Don't exchange glory for domestication; don't give up on the glory of the human animal for a set of ideas.

The Honourable Witness

The back story is this: in her rage, Laura had spat at the small boy and called him a racist name. She wasn't that angry with him personally, but he was the last straw after a difficult day.

When she told her husband, Malcolm, he wasn't quite sure what to do. Should he tell the truth or side with Laura and lie, hoping the small boy wouldn't be believed?

He asked around for advice. The priest said he should keep quiet, as his first obligation was to his sacred marriage vows. His friend said he should keep quiet, as charity began at home. His boss said he should keep quiet, as reputation was important.

When the police came round, Malcolm was ready.

'I saw it all,' he said, 'and nothing happened to the boy.'

So the boy wasn't believed and Laura and Malcolm celebrated another wedding anniversary – oh, and Malcolm's promotion at work!

Truth is too awkward for most people.

'What Are You Doing Now?'

The interviewer had a question for the TV celebrity.

'We don't see you on TV so much these days.'

'That's true.'

'All those outrageous interviews you used to do, savagely exposing people! You don't seem to be doing them now.'

'No, I'm not.'

'But why not? It's what you do!'

'In the end, I had to reflect on my own self and I found I was quite as absurd as those I made fun of.'

'Really?'

'Yes, really.'

'So what are you doing now?'

'You live the first half of your life creating a mask; you live the second half of your life peeling it away. That's what I'm doing now.'

The Unmarked Tins

'Johnny, what have you done in the kitchen?!'

'What do you mean?'

'I can't find anything! I mean, what's in this tin?! Peaches? Tomato soup? Mushy peas? How am I supposed to know? It's hopeless! And you just back from a spiritual retreat!'

'I had to do it, Mother.'

'Oh, you did, did you?!'

'Yes, I did.'

'And why is that?'

'The guru was very clear: the first act of insight is to throw away all labels.'

Labels — for kitchens, but not for life.

4

The Formless Way

The Blank Canvas

For something good to happen, we need to create space. Whether we are launching a rocket, playing tennis, holding a party or receiving a new sofa, we need to create space for the event. It's obvious. And it's also obvious that if we want something new or good to happen inside us, we need to clear some inner space for it.

I saw a terrible accident on the motorway recently. Some clutter falling from the back of a lorry turned the freeway into a pile-up of collision and twisted metal. Clutter in us has similar results. Life speeds towards us and, instead of passing cleanly through, hits our emotional debris. The outcome can be a disaster for everyone – not so much twisted metal as twisted relationships. And there are no nice men in fluorescent jackets to surround us with cones while everything is sorted.

One simple way to remove the crash clutter and create inner space is to imagine yourself as a blank canvas. You can do it now, wherever you are. All the angry, fearful or worried colours of yesterday are gone. There is just cream-white space, ready to receive whatever today brings.

Some painters fear the blank canvas; one even told me he doesn't exist when the canvas is empty: 'To contemplate that space is like attending my own funeral!' he moaned. But my sense is that life actually begins when we are blank, clean, like untouched snow in the playground, waiting for new footprints and games.

It's about Time

I spoke with a social worker recently, and it was about time. They told me how they had learned to compartmentalize their life so that no part impinged on any other part. 'I've built strong walls between them all!' they said with pride, as though it made them strong and professional. But I heard their words with sadness and sensed only defensiveness and fear. Why the need for walls? What were these dams holding back?

Some people do treat their day like a cake – they dig in the knife and slice it up in segments. Compartmentalize or die! This time is for this; that time is for that. Often, we even decide in advance which part of the day we will enjoy and which we won't, which part will draw kindness from us and which will draw only indifference or cruelty. 'I *will* like that! I *won't* like that!'

This slicing may give us a sense of control, but cuts horribly against the grain of truth. For time and self are one, and are best left as such. The day may offer different situations and ask of us different roles. But we are the same person beneath each role, and beneath the events, the day is the same – a seamless robe, an unboundaried stretch of sea.

It's about time we became one.

Written in Stone

If you come with me now, we could take a walk. I don't know how things are for you today, what thoughts and emotions crowd your life. You may not be very sure yourself, in which case could I suggest something? That you reflect on these things as we walk: what are you sad about? What are you happy about? With whom are you angry? And why?

We have a little way to go, but I hope you feel it's worth it.

Where are we headed? We're going to Ross-on-Wye, in search of two particular memorial stones, commemorations in stone of two lives lived in the flesh. They stand side by side, in death as in life, wife and husband.

We're nearly there now – how are you feeling? Is this a good day or not so good? Life is difficult, I know, but I sense in you a rather brave soul, so I don't fear for you.

Ah, here we are! And first, let's look at Margaret Potter's stone. Can you read the words there?

'All the way to heaven is heaven.'

And then if you look across to the stone next to it, that of Dennis Potter, there are some other words:

'And all of it a kiss.'

We don't need to rush away. There's really no rush at all. We have all the time in the world…

If God Were a Burglar

The International Labelling Laboratory (also known as ILL) divides everyone up by labelling them – again and again and again.

It labels black, white, gay, straight, religious, atheist and agnostic. It labels funny, sad, sane and mad, male and female, young and old…

Are you wearing your label? Or rather, your labels? Oh yes, everyone has a few.

ILL uses the labels to define people: friend or foe, good or bad, right thinking or wrong thinking, them and us. It makes very clear who's in, who's out and who should receive our favour today.

Unsure about that? Don't give it another thought. Just check the label provided by ILL – that will tell you everything you need to know about someone.

But wait a minute! Some breaking news! Oh no! Apparently last night someone broke into the laboratory and stole all the labels. This meant that this morning there was the shocking sight of people looking at other people without labelling them in any way. Crisis!

Who was it who broke into the label laboratory? The police don't yet know, but I have to say, if God were a burglar, this is just the sort of nonsense he'd steal…

A Revealing Interview

I recently caught up with Truth and in a revealing interview I asked what she did all day.

'I take form!' she said. 'I must always have shape!'

'But aren't you more of an idea?'

'Not at all! I take flesh; I look like something, feel like something!'

'How d'you mean?'

'Watch me! Watch me as I become a walrus, an oriental carpet or a stone at the bottom of the sea. I become all sorts of things – the school choir, religion, the street vendor, a car park, a sandwich or perhaps a desert dune!'

Truth went on to say that she adopted endless disguises, shrinking herself into many forms.

'I enjoy myself, I really do!' she said. 'I love all the dressing up!'

'And the problems?'

'No problems at all!' says Truth with a big smile. 'As long as people never mistake me for the form itself! I am the carpet but I am not the carpet. Not at all!'

A Consolation Prize

It's a pattern of sorts, if a rather messy and uncomfortable one.

A moment of illumination and discovery is often preceded by a period of distress or despair, whether in the arts, sciences or religion.

A problem is presented that seems quite insoluble to the psyche. A meltdown follows as the inner body adjusts to new conditions and requirements. There is white-water ferment in the soul until a solution emerges from the watery chaos, a 'Eureka!' moment. What could not be imagined before is imagined now; insight is given, understanding granted and much changed.

You have experienced these things, both the ferment and the joy.

Such ecstatic consolations will be temporary; we cannot maintain their intensity. But this is fine. We receive them; then let them go. We enjoy them as sweet friends on our journey, but don't allow them to calcify into dogma.

They point the way; they don't lock us in.

The Beautiful Vase

Do you have a beautiful vase in which you keep your truth?

Is it perhaps an ancient vase? One passed down by your parents? Or maybe one you discovered yourself?

Wonderful! What a precious thing it is! Holding all things for you, enjoying pride of place in your home.

So clearly you must take it outside now and smash it against the wall.

Because truth cannot be kept in formulas, whether ancient, family or your own. Like a slave on the run, truth dreads the deadening shackles of form, even the form of a beautiful vase.

Keep an eagle in a cage and it goes mad.

A Borrowed Life

The young man had come to this country to study. He was working part time in a store, but he'd come to get a degree.

It hadn't really been a choice. His father wished it and his father was a forceful man.

So he'd get a proper university degree. No one in his village had one of those. He was to be the first! The first man in the village with a degree!

And that's what his father wanted.

And so it was that he came to this country with second-hand dreams – dreams that were not his own.

And he lived a borrowed life, a life borrowed from his father's wardrobe, a vicarious existence, on behalf of someone else.

Which is a shame, because we were made to be original.

The Trouble with Do-Gooders

The trouble with do-gooders is their hatred. They seem to love two things: doing good and hating people.

There they are, busy being wonderful in support of a group of people and equally busy with hate for those who cause this group's suffering.

This is a problem, though, because if you hate on behalf of a good cause, your good cause turns bad. It is the self-righteous psyche in a nutshell and is neither attractive nor helpful.

So here's what I'm feeling in response to all this: no one who is happy creates suffering; only the unhappy do this. And neither is anyone all good or all bad; there are only speckled people on Earth, who display a bit of both.

So we shall hate no one, because it's not worthy of us. Instead, we shall somehow wish all beings well.

As the Dalai Lama said, before we find compassion, let us acquire impartiality.

The Rickety Clothes Line

Life is happier when we do not hope.

Hoping for things is like hanging clean washing on a rickety clothes line in a muddy field during a really terrible storm – it's nerve-wracking and tends to disappoint.

Hope makes us cling to outcomes and can make us rigid in approach.

It is probably enough to tend today's wounds and sing today's joys.

Tomorrow is better that way.

And surprisingly hopeful.

The Blind Elephant at Midnight

The taxi driver is telling me about himself.
He is Kenyan, apparently, only he isn't.
Confused? Then let me explain:
he is Somali by origin and regards Somalia as his homeland.
But the national boundaries,
drawn up by stupid foreigners in the last century,
make him Kenyan, even though he isn't!

It is frustrating when people put us in the wrong box,
but even more so, when we do it to ourselves.

As soon as I say: 'I am this!' or 'I am that! Or, 'I am the other!'
then I have lost my way –
like a blind elephant down a mine shaft at midnight,
on a very dark night.

There is no box. So why keep getting into it?

'Don't Paint the Table'

The art students gathered in the studio for their weekly class. There was keen anticipation. What would they be painting today?

Their teacher arrived, placed a table in front of them and said, 'Don't paint the table.'

There was surprise in the room. Having placed the table in front of them, why had the teacher said that? The students were also a little disappointed, since they could all paint tables. They'd done 'table painting' in Year 2 and considered themselves experts. So they asked the teacher what they should paint, if it wasn't to be the table.

'Paint what you see,' said the teacher. 'If you paint what you see, a table might emerge, a real and truthful table. If you paint what you imagine you see, then we have just another dull fantasy, the fantasy of what you think a table should look like.'

This, of course, is why the convinced are often so dull. They are so sure they know about life, they have given up looking at it. The wise know nothing, look at everything ... and paint what they see.

Too Much Tomb Soon

It is a shame if we reach our tomb too soon;
if we build a coffin for ourselves while still in our prime;
though, as we know, it does happen.

People search for security in the world;
they want meaning, a sure and certain place,
but seek it by closing things down rather than opening things
up.

They wall themselves in, cramped but held,
and then ask someone to nail down the lid!

'Safe at last!' they proclaim, lying trapped in the darkness.

Who can say when a groove becomes a grave, or a belief
becomes a box?

Buried aged 83; died aged 31.

The Walking Dead

We would do well to remember that we are only occasionally alive – only occasionally alive to ourselves and the world around us. If we remember to remember this, we may be spared the madness of self-importance.

Generally, the opposite is true – we are the dead going about our business, vague ghosts in a world of solids. We hobble along in the chains of our history and wear the blinkers of our unexamined past. We mutter from our dreams and declare from our hallucinations, but little of sense comes out, for we are dead folk walking – and talking to those like ourselves.

So we will remember that only occasionally are we aware; only occasionally alive to the world's colour, light and scents; to our fortune, resilience and joy; to the magnificent creatures who people our way.

And only occasionally alive to our space within, which holds all things but grips none.

Fragile

The year 1869 was turning out to be a very good one for Gustave Flaubert, the French author most famous for his novel *Madame Bovary*. In a letter to a friend, penned in this year, he was happy with life. And why not? After all, he didn't know what was round the corner.

Five weeks after he had written the letter, his friend Louis Bouilet died, and shortly after that the critics turned on Flaubert's latest work. Soldiers occupied his house during the war of 1870, and that year also saw the death of another friend, Jules Duplan. Then 1872 bought both the death of his mother, with whom he lived, and the collapse of timber prices, which ruined him financially. Under such strain, his health, never good, finally cracked. By 1875 he was a broken man.

However determined or gifted we may be, life, like china in the hand, is a fragile thing. And that's OK.

Spiritual Materialism

Spiritual materialism, a phrase coined by Chogyam Trungpa, is what happens when we ask our ego to look after our search for truth.

Our ego doesn't panic at the request, merely adopts the spiritual teaching for its own ends. 'From here on, you will be known as someone spiritually mature!' it says, proudly separating you from the common herd of humanity and setting you on a new treadmill of effort.

It is delighted with your desire for spiritual advancement and more than content to entertain itself with this new toy – until it gets irritating, of course. In the meantime, it will absorb nothing of consequence, ensuring no change, but will allow you to imitate spiritual practice, to give the impression of striving, advance and status.

True spirituality, on the other hand, quietly dismantles the ego's management of our journey, evaporating its grasp like sun on a damp pavement.

Asking the ego to look after our search for truth is like asking a wolf to look after our babies.

On Waking Up

An enquirer once questioned Buddha.

'Are you a god?' he asked.

'No, I am not a god,' came the reply.

'Then are you a spirit?'

'No, I am not a spirit.'

'Are you a man?'

'No, I am not a man.'

'Then what are you?'

'I am awake.'

Waking up has its attractions. What it must be to possess within yourself a deep reservoir of kindness, courage, curiosity, initiative, will, openness, passion, balance, justice, contentment and generosity. Imagine it! For that's what it is to be awake.

But in truth, most groan at the thought of waking up. They turn off the alarm, pull the cover over their head and sink back into a deep and snoring sleep.

Waking up can wait a while.

The Sapling and the Fence

When a sapling is young and vulnerable, it is good to protect it. In my local park they put metal fences around saplings in their early days, when they are not yet strong enough to fend for themselves. When a sapling gets larger, however, it is best to remove the fence, otherwise it will damage the tree. The metal becomes embedded in the bark and poisons it. Instead of protecting the young tree, the fence now kills it, which isn't the idea at all.

You might say this is obvious, and you're right, of course. I mention it, however, because I have seen people do the opposite. I know it sounds ridiculous, but I have seen this: I have seen people cut down the growing tree because it's beginning to threaten the fence! Somewhere along the way, they've become more committed to the fence than the tree.

All of which reminds me that a rule has only one reason for existence: to protect a beautiful attitude. The fence exists for the tree, not the tree for the fence.

A Lack of Lines

No lines now on the road;
no thick paint of white and yellow instruction;
no large neon-lit signs indicating how many miles to go;
no arrows clearly pointing;
no warnings of 'Big bend ahead'.

No insurance for your valuables;
no 'money back guarantee';
no 'on arrival' leaflets, or destination described.

No information desk; no uniformed people who know;
no knowing at all, save the speaking branches,
and the changing, chatting path,
which on occasion takes you aside to whisper the way –

the way of your journey, which carries you along
like a paper boat in the breeze.

The Path

I watched my friend walk along the path and noticed that sometimes, quite suddenly, he would break out into laughter. I couldn't see what was so funny, so I called out: 'Why do you laugh?'

'How could I do anything else?' he said. 'Look at me! I am so riddled with pretences, how could I possibly take myself seriously? No, I must laugh.'

Then a little later along the same path, I noticed that my friend was a frustrated figure in obvious despair.

I couldn't see why this should be so, so I called out: 'Why do you despair?'

'How can I do anything else?' he said. 'Look at me! What do you see but a tight little knot of self-protection? Of course I must despair!'

I watched him walk on down the path, laughing, despairing, laughing, despairing – and sometimes dancing.

Slightly worried, I asked a local woman where the path went.

'Oh, he'll be all right,' she said. 'It's the path to sanity.'

5
The Dark Night

Human Resources

I remember an old Western. A train was steaming across the desert, being chased by Indians. The immediate trouble was this: the people on the train were running out of wood to fuel it. Normal stocks had been used up.

'We're done for!' said the boy.

'No, we're not,' said the driver.

'But we've no more wood!'

'We have plenty of wood.'

'I don't see any!'

'Then get down to those carriages!'

So the boy went to the carriages and discovered wood. He smashed up tables and chairs and took them back to the front.

'I told you we had wood!' said the driver, filling the fire and feeling the power.

As with the boy on the train, we sometimes believe our supplies to have run out. We feel spent, with no more to offer, yet this is usually an illusion.

At such times, instead of despairing, call on fresh supplies from unlikely places. Seek out every sinew and joint in your body; call down the corridors of artery and vein; insist on depth from your breath and insight from your being. Invite the three keen energies of head, heart and gut into the room and demand a response from them all! Your train has many miles in it yet.

The Busy Bodyguard

The dancer was wonderful – such grace and beauty on stage. But she was considered too vulnerable amid the push, rush and threat of city life and was therefore given a bodyguard to look after her and ensure her safety.

The bodyguard was very good and it seemed an ideal arrangement for everyone. He handled the dangers competently, planning routes and avoiding all difficult places.

'Don't you worry about a thing,' he said.

The downside was that the dancer got out much less; indeed, she was scarcely seen at all after a while. The bodyguard ran her errands and even went to meetings on her behalf.

You won't believe this, but after a few months he even started dancing instead of her! While the dancer sat alone, wondering what had gone wrong…

An Arrowing Experience

I remember a conversation with a friend. He'd been telling me how eager he was to grow as a person.

'I *so* want to grow!' he said.

I then noticed something sharp flying towards us.

'Can you see what I see?' I asked.

'What do you see?'

'There's an arrow flying through the air, aimed at you.'

'Really? Oh no! That's terrible!'

'No cause for alarm,' I said.

'Why ever not? I'm very alarmed!'

I could see his point, but wished to reassure him that he had nothing to fear. 'The arrow is from God,' I said.

'Oh, well, that's a relief! I thought for a moment I had an enemy out there!'

'No, you're fine. There's no enemy firing at you.'

'Phew!'

'The arrow will kill you of course—'

'Kill me? But I don't want to die!'

'Oh, I'm sorry, I must have misunderstood. I thought you wanted to grow as a person!'

The Field of Flowers

Today we discover some men tasting freedom after a long period of captivity. It must surely be the happiest day of their lives. We are in the final days of World War Two, outside the bleak walls of a concentration camp, recently liberated. The captors have gone and the inmates, free at last, have been allowed out for a walk. Suddenly, they find themselves standing in a field of wonderful flowers. What joy they must feel! When did they last see anything like this? But instead of joy, they make a sobering discovery: despite the beauty, they can find no feelings for the flowers.

In the evening, back in their huts, they talk amongst themselves about their experiences.

'Tell me,' says one of them, to his friend, 'were you pleased today?'

'Truthfully?'

'Truthfully.'

'No,' he said.

Brutalized by circumstances, they had lost the ability to be pleased, as Victor Frankl recalls. For although their bodies were liberated, their spirit was not. Happiness, taken from them so savagely, was something they had to relearn slowly, and some would never make it.

'Step by step I progressed, until I again became a human being,' records Frankl.

He speaks for many whose lives are rising slowly out of the ashes.

Down at the Sorting Office

Here are two parcels you will need to claim from the sorting office.

You will collect your hot package of anger and sit with it for a while. Let any self-righteous rage or wild fury give way to simple anger, specific to your memory and experience. You have not always been well served by others, particularly when you were small and vulnerable. You must claim what you feel before you can give it away.

And you will also collect your damp package of sadness and sit with it for a while. Let any melodramatic sense of tragedy or vague despondency give way to simple sadness, specific to your memory and experience. Things have not been as you hoped they might be in your brief stay on Earth. You must claim what you feel before you can give it away.

And this is the thing. Once collected and unwrapped, anger and sadness can become something; until then, a part of us is rotting in the sorting house.

The Old Raft

Buddha thought that just because a raft
had got us across a piece of water,
enabling us to continue our journey,
it didn't mean we had to carry that raft on our back
for the rest of our lives.

He felt that we carried many things
that had stopped being useful.
They had served us once, that's for sure;
but they did so no longer,
because circumstances had changed.

In fact, they hindered us now, because they were heavy;
and could not do what we needed to be done.

So, on reflection, I have decided to throw away the life belt
that saved me in the flood.
I had been hoping it would fly me to the moon,
but it shows little sign of that.

I may need something else to get me there.

Absence

When the little boy has been told his dad is coming to take him out on Saturday, it is very hard when he doesn't turn up. His mum may try and console him; his dad may even ring to say he hopes to come next week instead. But really, such things do not make up for the experience of being let down, of being reckoned unimportant, of painful absence.

If such experiences are repeated again and again, they form thick layers of despair and distrust in the child. Too young to question, the hurt simply lodges, unexpressed, in the boy's body.

He needs to be able to ask why. He needs to be able to shout his pain. Like Jesus, in fact, when he hung crucified on his cross and screamed into the evening sky: 'My God, my God, why have you forsaken me?!'

One mystic famously spoke of 'the dark night of the soul'; others have talked of a 'crisis of meaning.' Whatever we call such times, they will come to the mystic, and there is no grand way to handle them. They are not the end of the story – far from it. But that is how they feel, ripping us up into a thousand pieces, and each piece a pain.

Like a night traveller, we search the skies for the dawn…

After the Flood

When the dam was built and the river valley flooded, many of the old settlements were lost. Houses and homes, lived in for centuries, disappeared; family stories were submerged and whole ways of life destroyed. It was terrible.

Life moves on; change happens. But it's hard losing loved and familiar things and then having to get on with life as if all is well. The flood comes in wet savagery and everything is changed. We don't know what to do.

It's like Santa getting up on Christmas morning to deliver the presents, only to discover it's already been done. It's such a shock! What does he do now? When doing presents at Christmas is all he's ever known?!

After the flood, however it comes, there's nothing but shock, anger, panic, sadness — oh, and new life growing. The children sail in the valley now, and Santa? He loves his new job in the care home.

Whether or Not to Answer

I won't be keeping you long today.
I need to get on, and I'm sure you do too.
And anyway, often less is more.

It's just that when a strong emotion comes beating on your door,
disturbing you terribly,
it's best to answer it and see who it is.

We can be upset by the hammering and the shouting,
and, with ear plugs in place, attempt to ignore it.

But such callers are less frightening for being spoken with,

and always leave when understood.

The Strawberry

How did you get into this situation?

You're being chased by a tiger and have been doing pretty well. Only now you've reached the edge of a cliff. Do you go forward or back?

There's no choice, because the tiger is closing in behind you, so you grab a vine and, holding tight, begin to shin down the rock face.

It's then you realize that it's worse than you thought. There's another tiger, equally large, waiting for you at the bottom, and not only that – a mouse is chewing at the vine that is supporting you.

Caught between these two killer cats – one at the top, the other at the bottom – and with a mouse gnawing at your security, you notice a strawberry growing on the cliff face.

It's red and ready, and so you eat it.

Wonderful! Perhaps the best strawberry you have ever tasted.

They do say that the origin of happiness is to be able to live in the moment.

After the Strawberry

Not everyone knows what happened after you ate the strawberry.

So here's telling:

The vine breaks and you fall towards the tiger waiting at the bottom of the cliff. As you fall, you curse the mouse who has brought you to this by gnawing through your vine. If that wretched mouse hadn't chewed away your support, you wouldn't now be plummeting towards a terrifying tiger.

And then suddenly the tiger is gone! It is running away, making for the bush – but why?

You hear a noise – and then you understand. The mouse has fallen, too, and in scuttling about has frightened the tiger. Tigers hate mice.

The mouse who destroyed you has now saved you.

Indeed, they were the only one who could. Without that mouse, you'd still be hanging, safe but hopeless, in between two hungry tigers.

Sometimes a curse is a blessing.

You Didn't Read This

There is a place within us too painful to go to.

It's hard to find and well-protected. Most of our experiences in life don't take us anywhere near it. Indeed, they take us away from it, and with good reason.

We knew the way there once, but no more; once we had the keys to the door, but we threw them away. Who'd want keys to that door?

The paths to it are now secret and even its existence widely denied.

'I don't know of any such place,' we say, hurrying off to their lodgings in the wall of silence. 'And anyway, it destroys all who enter!'

It's ruthlessly protected. But should the defences be breached, the rumour is that you enter an inner room of endless softness, vulnerability and pain.

This is the talk on the street, and it has the ring of truth. And I've seen some who've stumbled upon that place and left laughing.

Suffering Fools

Do you find suffering upsetting?
    I find suffering upsetting.
    Suffering asks the question: 'Who are you?'
    And this is why I am so upset –

because most of me is phoney.

'And This Isn't the News'

And now for the news about why the news today will be bad, with more of the same tomorrow:

It takes a long time to build a ship, but little time to sink it. So for every 'Ship built' headline, there can be a hundred announcing: 'Ship sunk'.

The building of a ship is complex, involving many people in many different ways over a long period of time, whereas the sinking of a ship is more straightforward and instantly grasped.

The building of the ship is planned and expected; the sinking of the ship is surprising and unexpected, so has shock value. The expected is not news.

Oh – and here's a thing: people like bad news. There's something in us that seeks out bad things to distract us from our own uncomfortable selves. A ship sunk at sea? Excellent! Someone to blame at last! Something to tut-tut about!

As for us, however, we remain shipbuilders and adventurers on the high seas, unsunk by a diet of bad news.

When the Rain Came

How the rain fell!
How the skies opened in a deluge of wet!
Lightning flashed, thunder rumbled,
and the water came in sheets,
like wind-whipped airborne tides,
lashing the pavement,
and halting cars in the torrential assault.

And the road itself?
The tarmac was a river of tears.
The shocked road was drowning,
gasping for breath, awash with the wet,
overwhelmed and overcome by circumstance.

I watched in horror. I knew how the road felt.

Name and Shame

It was one of the most remarkable observations of all time, as much for its setting as for the words themselves.

Pain was exploding in his brain as the metal pins did their savage work. They had planned this. Three years of hate and jealousy, sniping and fear from every angle, poisoning everything positive. But now they had him, and with the backing of both the mob and the courts.

So they'd won and he'd lost. End of story. And with the nailing done, the cross was swung skywards by the soldiers. Now was the time for the man to speak his mind about this injustice; now was the time for Jesus to name and shame, surely? Here goes, hear this!

'Father, forgive them – they don't know what they are doing.'

What does he mean? Don't know what they're doing? They'd planned this for three years, hadn't they?!

The unconscious do terrible things in their sleep...

The Embarrassing Photo

I take a photo from the box and immediately regret my choice. It's a picture of a little boy with no front teeth, picking his nose. He has a stupid know-it-all smirk and ill-fitting clothes he somehow imagines are cool.

It is me long ago, once upon a time. I've grown up now, of course, made my way in the world – and thank God for that! But how embarrassing all the same. Behold this little figure enthroned at the centre of his own pathetic universe, and really quite ugly.

I hastily put the leper back in the box. I bury him beneath a hundred other prints. Move on, move on!

Though until I can befriend that leper, I can befriend no one.

The mystic embraces what they were, what they became, what they are and what they will be. All these are most lovingly held.

What's It Worth?

A book called *Practical Mysticism*, written by Evelyn Underhill, was published in 1914, as Britain stepped into the turmoil and tragedy of World War One. It became a popular book and is still available today. At the time, however, there was much debate in the publishing house that produced it. Should they postpone its publication until the destruction and agony were over? Some people felt that mysticism was a self-indulgence, a spiritual plaything best held back for sweeter times.

In the end, they decided to publish. If mysticism couldn't forge a strong spiritual vision that could 'transcend, hold and enfold the nightmare', then really, what was it worth? If it wasn't true here and now amid the slaughter, then it wasn't true amid any peace and laughter to come.

A mystic is one who has seen a curtain drawn back on their world and lives now not in one world but two. No hardship is removed, but light spills and penetrates as two worlds meet.

Well Done

This morning I'm drawing from a familiar well.
I'm lowering the bucket down into the darkness,
just as I always do.

I've drawn from it often,
but though the rope used to be long enough,
these days I'm not so sure.
I seem to get less water every time I come here!

And last Thursday I got none – nothing at all.
There was a little bit on Friday, but there's been nothing since.
And the bucket is empty again today.

I'm beginning to wonder if I need to move on.
I don't want to, but what served me once is serving me no
longer.

Clearly all is not well.

The Kindness of Aunt Celia

Aunt Celia had always been Jean's favourite aunt and the best place to go when things were hard. Perhaps she was just one of life's kind people. What a quaint and easy life she must have had!

So it came as a great shock to Jean when one day she heard of Aunt Celia's past sorrows.

'I never realized,' she said.

'Oh yes, deep sadness, I'm afraid. Quite threw me at the time; I had nothing to put up against it. All I could do was feel sorry for myself and cry.'

'But you've always been so kind!'

'Not so. But if I became kind, I suspect I have sadness to thank.'

'Don't say that, Aunty!'

'It's true, my dear. Kindness springs from sorrow, from knowing there's nothing else but to dissolve the pain into consideration for others.'

A Cross with a View

What you learn, when hanging on a cross, is not to wriggle too much, not to wrestle. It's no help, and doesn't set you free; instead, it just increases the pain where the nails are biting.

Instead, you accept it and begin to realize that hoisted high, you have quite a view. You certainly see things you haven't seen before. You also become aware that gathered around you are one or two friends who are here for one reason and one reason only: you live in their heart.

You cry, yes, and scream. This union with nails is not a union you would have chosen.

But then sometimes you find yourself laughing and believing – believing that someday someone might come and take you down.

And that every union is a path for the taking and not the end of the road.

6

The Still, Small Voice

A Country Garden Observed

I was surveying the garden on a lazy summer's day. All colour and spilling blossom! But how exactly was it watered?

First I saw a man at a well, heaving up water with a bucket and laboriously pouring it on the land.

Then, in another part of the garden, I noticed a sprinkler: easier than well-and-bucket, but still needing relocation from time to time.

And then there was a little stream, wending its jaunty way through vegetable patch and flower beds.

Oh, and the rain of course! It arrived without warning and had me leaping out of my chair. Quite unpredictable in its force, but soaking the garden as nothing else could for a couple of hours.

Later, I returned to the garden and reflected on the different types of watering. The active watering from the well and sprinkler, requiring work. And the passive watering of stream and rain, requiring no work.

The mystic knows there are things they can do to help themselves. But sometimes help is just a gift, like a stream running through us or sudden life-softening rain.

Feeding the Ducks

I walked with my friend to the pond in the park. It was a bright sunny day at the start of spring, just the sort of day to feed the ducks.

Only when we got there, the ducks didn't want to be fed! I threw them bread and they turned their backs!

'Perhaps they're full,' said my friend. 'There are a lot of other people feeding them today.'

'Well, maybe,' I said, 'but they could still be polite and show some interest! I mean, we've come all this way!'

And then one of the passing ducks stopped and looked at me.

'Where were you in January?' asked the duck.

'January?' I said, surprised in so many ways.

'Yes, January,' said the duck. 'I didn't see you here then.'

'But it was freezing in January!' I said. 'Really cold!'

'Exactly,' said the duck, before waddling off towards the jetty.

We stood in silence for a while.

'Well, what was all that about?' I asked.

'Our self-love posing as charity?' suggested my friend.

Separated in the Crowd

Sometimes we have a need to be reunited with our loveliness, for someone or something to bless us into fresh-as-dew awareness of our simple wonder.

How might it happen?

It might come quietly and impossibly, like seeds flowering in dry land. Or it might come powerfully, like a strong tide washing deckchairs and sandcastles away.

Or perhaps it will come like this: like an old man meeting his childhood self. Imagine it! Imagine an old man, harshly treated by life, in conversation with the hopeful boy he once was – young, bright, miraculous and vital! Separated by the years, separated by experience, yet not separate at all. They are not two but one.

And we are one with our loveliness and wonder – though sometimes we get separated in the crowd.

An Unexpected Apology

It was not an apology I'd been expecting. Surely it was meant to be the other way round? It was certainly a shock.

For this was not me saying sorry to God, but God saying sorry to me! And you could have knocked me over with a feather.

It was all wrong, I knew that. The correct procedure was well-drilled into me: I say sorry to Him. I fall on my knees in shame and repent of my 'grievous sins': 'I'm so sorry, God!'

But it wasn't like that, not at all. Instead, here was God saying sorry to me: 'I apologize for all you've been through, I really do. How can I make it up to you?'

At first I didn't know where to put myself. I wasn't sure how things could be made right.

I just knew they would be – and that's made all the difference.

Morning Worship

Every morning I walk through the park.

It's a small city park but well kept. It's different throughout the year, of course, depending on the season. It rests in the winter and comes to life in spring. There's a constant adjustment to circumstance, whether snowy, sunny, blustery or wet.

I have wanted to say thank you to the gardeners for a long time; they may not know how much I appreciate their work. And yesterday I did, halting a gruff man with a lawnmower to speak my gratitude. Irritation in his eyes became surprise and then pride; it is possible no one had said thank you before.

Though today I was sad, because the gates were locked and I couldn't pass through my park. I peered over the hedge from the pavement, but felt the exclusion.

We all have our holy places.

The Daily Conversation

The Sufi mystic Rumi invited us to consider ourselves as a guest house. Each morning there would be a new arrival – whether a joy, a depression or a meanness.

He said we should welcome and entertain all arrivals, regardless of their beauty, and be grateful for whoever appeared, for each had been sent as a guide from beyond.

This reminds me of St Francis seeing a slug and greeting it with the words: 'Welcome, Brother Slug – and what message do you bring for me today?'

Life is a conversation with the world around us and within us. If we inch ourselves back from centre stage and pay attention to each arrival on the scene, a dialogue begins; we both speak and are spoken to.

We could scarcely be less alone.

The Lion

I remember seeing him for the first time and feeling unsettled.

The caged lion was sitting subdued, being fed rubbish by the keepers. Whatever it was born to eat, this wasn't it. And I have to say it looked cold in the wind, its shaved mane scattered round about, cut for health and safety reasons. It was important to be clean in public.

The lion was a popular attraction with the visitors; most people took a look. 'Here's a lion who's safe!' said the sign, which made it good for families.

But here was also a sad lion, a lion whose eyes betrayed something half-remembered but lost now. What was it? If only it could get it back...

The crowd gawp at the lion in silent discomfort, for they look in a mirror. They look at the lion but see themselves.

A Beautiful Ambush

It was an unexpected ambush.

The flowers began the assault,
leaping from the roadside and catching me quite unawares.
Daffodils, crocus, blossom –
each pressing blessing on me,
and not taking 'no' for an answer!

Then came the scents and fragrance,
released by recent rain,
elusive yet sweet in the air.

And after the scent, the big guns – a marauding mob of
buildings,
skylines and telegraph poles,
each with its own compelling story,
impossibly rich in detail and depth.

Even the old metal railing joined in the revelation!
And the battered blue door, peeling but strong,
and a plant pot fallen and smashed.

Really, I had to get inside or be quite overwhelmed
by this brilliant and bruising ambush of beauty.

'It's Curtains for You'

You find me considering my curtains, and you can join me if you wish.

They hang now on either side of my window. I can't remember how long I've had them or how many times I've opened and closed them. These are not things you record in your diary, not great events. They are just things you do.

So what is there to say that isn't entirely obvious? Nothing really.

Sometimes I close the curtains to keep the world out and allow for darkness, forgiveness and rest.

And sometimes I open the curtains and declare for light, hope and action.

Sweet closing, sweet opening – day after day, week after week, year after year.

And there was me thinking I never prayed.

That Healing Place

Thank you for joining me in my world and offering a safe place. That's really all I wish to say.

Thank you for stooping so low as to enter my front room and stand there with me while I showed you my little collection of pictures, memories, mistakes, triumphs and sadness.

Thank you for not being too eager to get home and for not telling me that life's like that and I'd better pull my socks up. And thank you for leaving your own pictures and memories at home, sensing they would crowd out mine. I'm grateful also that you didn't give me any advice. I found that really helpful.

When the wounds are hard to bear, we all need a gentle place, a place where the speaking is honest, the confusion acknowledged and the hurt bathed.

So thank you. You became that place for me.

A Business Meeting Ruined

It was the end of the business meeting; we never quite got back on track after that.

We'd been sitting there discussing important business when we heard a scream. We rushed to the window to see a child in the street below, beating on a front door. She'd been locked out by an angry adult and was now alone and terrified, little hands hammering in helplessness at the door, shut out and scared.

After a while, an adult opened the door and the child was taken inside. We returned to our places around the table, ready to resume our important business. But it wasn't the same; we were no longer a business meeting, we were a community.

It's terrible to witness, but few inspire love in the world like the helpless do. And maybe one day I'll be the helpless one, ruining business meetings and creating surprising warmth in cold places.

In the Darkest Undergrowth

Amid the torrential rain within,
and the jerky gusts of wind,
in the darkest undergrowth of my sodden soul,
I was surprised and then amazed and then stunned
to find a candle burning.

This was not a candle I had lit or knew of;
nor had I protected it against the downpour.
It was just a candle I discovered,
burning away without a care in the world.

It was a home sign,
a sign of coming home –

like a light in the porch greeting a weary traveller.

Humpty Has a Fall

Humpty Dumpty sat on a wall,
Humpty Dumpty had a great fall
All the king's horses and all the king's men
Couldn't put Humpty together again.

Which in a way is just as well,
for he is better with his seal broken,
better with his shell cracked,
for now light shines through Humpty:
shines in
and shines out.
If there are no cracks, this doesn't happen.

He's cursing his eggs-asperating luck, of course; it feels so
severe.

But a severe mercy perhaps.

'Water, Water!'

I've heard many stories about the thirsty searching for water. Often such tales are set in the sweltering desert – ripping yarns of endurance beneath the midday sun, frail humans against the elements, no happy ending guaranteed.

'Water, water!' the thirsty croak, dragging themselves through the boiling sand. 'I need a drink! Water!'

This scenario has produced many great stories. Though I first became interested in the spiritual life when I experienced it turned on its head – a story in which the water searched for the thirsty.

'The thirsty!' gasps the cool water, flowing full and free. 'Where are they? Show me the thirsty! Let me give them drink!'

What a refreshing twist to an old tale.

Where Truth Comes From

There is nothing to be acquired as a mystic, no secret knowledge. Enlightenment arises not through clever teaching but through letting go. Truth emerges as gradually we throw overboard all the unhelpful psychological patterns that keep us from reality – from our true selves.

Letting go may make us scared; it may even make us cry. But it will also make us happy, for nothing good or lovely is lost, and much is gained. We are like people emerging from under a rubbish dump, suddenly free to breathe. Fresh answers emerge as old answers are given to the four winds.

And you knew this before you read it.

Why People Like the Clown

'Why do people like me?' asks the clown. 'Is it because I make them laugh?'

'They enjoy laughing, certainly,' says his friend.

'Or is it my colourful clothes, large shoes and big smile?'

'They enjoy those too.'

'But you don't think they're the real reason?'

His friend pauses –

and then speaks.

'The real reason why people like you is this: you always get up.'

'How d'you mean?'

'Whatever crisis has occurred, however hard you've been knocked over or sent tumbling, you always get up! With you, the story's never over. Whatever the disaster, the story gets up and goes on.'

'I suppose that's right.'

'More than the funny man, you're the resurrection man. And if it's true for you, it might be true for me as well. That's why we like the clown.'

Your Story

It's important your life emerges as your story, as opposed to someone else's; that a real person emerges from beneath the layers of conformity pressed upon you from within and without.

To this end, the Mexican voice of Miguel Ruiz suggests four simple acts:

1. Be honourable in your speech: the words you let loose have remarkable power to create both good and bad realities in the world.

2. Take nothing personally: do not digest other people's emotional bile.

3. Assume nothing: your fear of not knowing leads you to invent answers to your questions about situations. This false knowledge may temporarily reassure, but leads you into a particular form of hell.

4. Do your best: don't worry about imperfection, just enjoy the adventure of reclaiming yourself from the daily dream of conformity. Give it your best shot.

Four acts for living.

Mr P. Stone

You find me considering the city pavement. I'm sensing it must be quite hard to be a paving stone. All those people who walk over you every day, oblivious and busy, stopping only to drop litter on your face. Is the chewing gum the worst? I think it could be, the way it sticks and hardens dirt black. And I don't envy you the cold, either, or the lack of thanks you receive.

But then there are the good times, I suppose, when the rush stops and all is quiet. Do you talk with the other stones then? And sometimes the rain washes, the sun warms and there's that nice man with the broom to sweep, tickle and clean. That must feel very good indeed.

I'm the better for my union with Mr P. Stone. There's much we share.

An Exhausting Country Lane

I had a problem of gratitude on my run today – just too much of it!

I was away from home, running down a quiet country lane, when I noticed some forget-me-nots by the side of the road, which reminded me of my youth. So I said, 'Thank you,' as I ran, for they had been long-time companions on this planet.

Further on, I noticed some dandelions growing, a wonderful yellow in the breaking dawn, and I said thank you to them as well.

And then the primroses. How could I not say thank you to them? Or the bluebells, so vibrant this year, and lining my path for 50 yards like a cheering crowd, a fanfare of trumpets!

'Thank you! Thank you!' I said.

And then I noticed the hedge – home for the sparrow and windbreak for the flowers. 'Thank you!' I said to the hedge, who I suspect was a little surprised, because people didn't usually say that to him.

I haven't mentioned the cowslips swaying, or the milkman's smile, or the kind tarmac road which carried me along. But I don't wish my gratitude to be as exhausting for you as it was for me.

7

The Common Round - No Trivial Task

The Hardest Thing in the World

Some people say a diamond is the hardest thing in the world, but I'm not sure it is. I think the hardest thing in the world is to stand in someone else's shoes, enter into their world. Now that's what I call celebrity! To sense, for instance, the feelings of a mother losing a child at 22 weeks, or to know how a flower experiences the gentle rays of the summer sun, or understand the distant eyes in the street-hard youth.

So the hardest thing in the world is to be a mystic. Because a mystic gets up in the morning, cleans their teeth, trips over the dog and attempts this union with reality – attempts to stand in the shoes of the world. Mystics live not just in their own little world but in all the little worlds around them as well.

You will probably be a mystic today at work – and I don't mean sitting in the corner of the office, wearing a pointy hat. It may in fact mean nothing more than momentarily trying to understand the needs of another, who struggles like you but struggles differently. And can therefore appear entirely obnoxious.

A young man did once stand in my shoes – a new pair of trainers in fact. But he was running away, and wasn't a mystic – just a thief.

Studio Secrets

Sometimes, in old dramas, the young painter in the village is presented as rather effete and witless; all cravat, daydreams and tousled hair. Loved by the older women, tolerated by the vicar – but don't ask him to mend your plumbing!

In my experience, however, painters are just the opposite: supremely practical people who know what it takes to make a painting. So they know about hiring studios, choosing brushes, making the paint, making the frame, stretching the canvas across the frame, mixing colour, preparing the surface, assessing the light, dealing with the gallery and organizing transport for the finished product – alongside the small matter of the painting itself.

The painting we enjoy in the gallery is the result of many things: attention to practical detail; mental and physical work; shafts of inspiration and honed artistic skill. And time, of course, for these things take time, and struggle, for the painting never quite ends up like the original vision – there is constant crisis and constant adjustment.

To destroy the beautiful is easy, requiring only carelessness, malice or greed. But to create the beautiful, as the painter knows, requires practical and persistent engagement with many different realities.

Mystics will understand.

Two People Talking
for a Change

There are many different approaches to psychiatry, many different camps, each with their own guru.

They differ amongst themselves about how people can be changed. But what's really transforming is something they all share, and that's two people talking.

When all the clever theories of human development are put to one side, there remains this: the offer of a safe haven for dialogue. Here, the client is removed from the troubles of the world and held in some manner, like a happy child – accepted, heard and free to speak and grow.

Change is about two people talking and the mystic is part of this daily flow of healing conversation. It can happen anywhere – bus, home, work, bedside, canteen, airport, park, shop or street. Wherever two people greet each other, change is possible.

It's about a safe place, about being heard and being accepted.

It's about two people talking.

'I Have Met the Messiah!'

'I have met the messiah!' she told me.

'Why d'you say that?'

'If you saw him, you'd know what I mean!'

To be honest, I don't have much time for grandiose religious announcements, but, curious, I did go back with her to the place where she'd seen him. I was interested to get a glimpse, at least.

While waiting for the grand arrival, I watched a minibus pull up. The driver was a fat bald man who parked up and then went round to the back of the vehicle to help disabled children out. He smiled a lot and was patient, because it took a while. He made them laugh with his jokes and they went happily off to school.

With the diversion over, I returned to the messiah watch.

'So where is he, then?' I asked.

'Don't be stupid. You've just been watching him!'

'What – the bald fat man?'

'Wonderful, isn't he? Isn't it great how he cares for people?'

'Yes, but he's hardly the messiah!'

'Well, if he's not the messiah, he's someone very like him.'

A Living Legend

Darrol found me on the shop floor to ask about some missing paperwork.

I had responsibility for the newspapers and magazines. I put them out each day and returned unsold copies from the day before. Darrol handled the documentation that came with them. We worked as a team.

I told him I'd left the paperwork by the computer, about half an hour ago. He said he couldn't see it, so we went together to find it. I discovered it quite quickly. It was in the bin.

'Well, here it is,' I said, adding a little defensively, 'but I didn't put it there.'

'You know what?' said Darrol. 'I think I did! What was I thinking?!'

Well, I was dumbstruck at the mysticism!

Darrol could easily have pretended someone else had done it: 'Honestly! Which idiot put it there? Some people!'

But he didn't. He took responsibility for what he'd done; he engaged honestly with his own reality.

Darrol is a living legend in the annals of mystic adventures.

Road Drill

We sat together in her small flat.

Another pensioner with time on her hands, Edna was worried by the road drilling outside. I wasn't surprised. She had lived with it daily for the past two weeks, a relentless and nerve-jangling reverberation that made even conversation difficult. It would have driven me to despair, possibly violence.

'I don't know how you put up with it,' I said.

'Oh, it's not *me* I'm worried about,' she replied, with a dismissive wave of her hand. 'It's the poor man with the drill.'

'The man with the drill?'

'Well, fancy doing that for a job! I only have the racket for a few weeks; he has it every day of his life!'

'I suppose so,' I said, struggling to sound concerned.

Love is putting yourself in someone else's shoes, even when they have a drill in their hands.

The Little Hill That Roared

After the Amazon and the Nile, the Yangtze is the third longest river in the world. Starting in the glaciers of Tibet and travelling across China to the region of Shanghai, it is called 'the Long River' by the Chinese.

But it might have been lost to them. A hundred miles south of Batang, the river is heading out of China towards Thailand and Cambodia when it meets a hill and returns north.

It's not a big or famous hill, and nothing compared to some of the mountains around it. But alone it halts the mighty river in its tracks, turning the flow northwards on a nation-defining journey across China.

I suspect the hill may have been put there by the god of small things, who exists because nothing else matters.

Scribbles from Chuang Tzu's Notebook

Enjoy your work and the changing seasons.

Avoid grand plans; just respond to things as they arise.

Push your own self to one side, as far as you are able, so you can see other people more clearly.

And instead of seeking fulfilment, seek only to be empty. This will create space for true understanding.

Do not value power, but do value peace.

It's OK to swing between joy and sadness, glory and failure – there's no great difference between them.

Breathe slowly and listen for the order in the universe.

Making Light of Work

We shall do our work lightly; I sense this is best.
This is not to do it carelessly, with distracted attention,
nor lazily, because we simply can't be bothered,
nor superficially, because we fear going deeper,
nor restlessly, because we ache to get on with the next great
thing.
But lightly, with a feather touch that neither clings nor claims
too much.

For whatever we do, whatever our work, it's a role we adopt,
a game we play, not who we are.

Barry

You know what they say about Barry in the office and none of it's very polite:

- 'Room-temperature IQ, that one!'
- 'Bright as Alaska in December.'
- 'If brains were taxed, he'd get a rebate.'
- 'He must have got into the gene pool while the life guard wasn't watching.'
- 'Possesses the wisdom of youth and the energy of old age.'
- 'The evolutionary process clearly built a bypass round his house.'
- 'He reached rock-bottom long ago – and carried on digging.'
- 'The gates are down, the lights are flashing, but there's no train coming.'
- 'He's depriving some village of an idiot.'

Well, maybe. But I loved Barry. He was the only one who gave me tea when I made deliveries to his office...

Quite a Crowd!

On hearing I had a problem, Uncle Tom went straight into action. He was good like that. He loved doing things for people.

And in many ways, what he achieved with a few phone calls and e-mails was quite remarkable. Within the hour, he had the following on my doorstep: an electrician, a carpet salesman, a locksmith, a glazier, a car mechanic, two mountaineers, a horse breeder, a bishop, some hairdressers, a commercial airline pilot, the All Blacks rugby team, a dog handler, five travel agents on a bonding exercise, a newly qualified ski instructor, a quiz-show host and a successful wine importer from Gwent.

As I say, it was remarkable in its way, though not that helpful for the unblocking of my drain. What I really needed was a plumber.

Love is the *accurate* assessment of need...

Small Things

Each day, we are given the strength to do small things, for our life is comprised of such events. There are no big things, just small things; small things well lived. Perhaps we do the washing up after supper, write a card, wonder about a holiday or invoice a client. Perhaps we build a wall, make a speech, drive up the motorway or go hospital visiting. Perhaps we e-mail a job proposal, make coffee for a colleague at work, pilot a plane over France or see a rainbow.

As I say, there are no big things, just small things; small things well lived daily. Tomorrow's small things remain a mystery, of course; a quiet unfolding way beyond our plans. Today's are enough, arriving like a string of pearls, one after the other.

As to what they'll become, who knows? Though I suspect these small things add up. As Van Gogh said: 'Great things are not done by impulse, but by a series of small things brought together.'

Taking Notice

I notice the clouds contain a hint of blue and orange;
I notice the street bin is full to bursting;
and that the passing bus is empty, not in service.
I notice a loose paving stone rocking beneath my feet;
and that I feel in a hurry today,
tense in my shoulders, my heart pumping.

I notice a sweet scent on the wind;
a brief feeling of optimism passing through me,
and some discarded takeaway boxes, with fried chicken
remains.

I notice the unseen roofs of houses;
a child's face at a small round window;
a car speeding past, fast and furious;
and I notice I'm angry with the driver.

I notice the newsagent putting out a sign,
at the beginning of her long, long day.

And I notice I'm alive — here, today, now.
Wow!

The Spiral Way

The way of the mystic is not a linear path. We do not slay dragons one after the other, proceeding in a clear chronological line towards fulfilment.

Neither is the mystic way a circle, a despairing and closed circuit in which we return again and again to the same experiences.

Rather, the way of the mystic is the spiral way – circular, but with ever-changing vistas. On the spiral way, we may visit old scenes, grapple with old dragons. But each time we return, we do so as different people and from a different place; the experience is not the same.

'I am here again, but I have never been here before.' The mystic may often say things like that on the spiral way.

Oh – and instead of slaying old dragons, they just view them differently.

Positive about the Negative

Q: What will I need to give up today?
A: Your negative emotions, which are unhelpful.

Q: How do I do that?
A: First, through self-observation, by beginning to notice when the negative appears. When it does, say something like: 'Ah, a negative emotion! Greetings!'

Q: *Greetings?*
A: Definitely. We don't need to be impolite to the negative, just notice it.

Q: OK. And then?
A: Once you've noticed it, refuse to identify with it. Say something like: 'You've called at my door, negative emotion. I understand why you've come, but I'm not letting you in. You're persuasive, but you only harm my space.'

Q: Easier said than done. Any practical tips?
A: Help yourself at the start of each day. Before the accidents of life are upon you, form within yourself a resistant space. Find a sacred room in yourself from which to face the changes and chances of this fleeting world.

Overall, be positive about the negative; it has positively no place in you.

The School Fool

Tomkinson was soon to leave the school and his teacher wanted a final word with him. He had never liked the boy, if he was honest. Indeed, on occasion it had given him pleasure to make his life a misery. He had not always used his power fairly perhaps, but then Tommo had played the fool too often.

And now time for some final words.

'Soon to leave, Tomkinson?'

'Soon to leave, sir, yes.'

'So tell me, what do you want to be when you grow up?'

'I'm not sure,' replied the boy. 'How about you, sir?'

We must never mistake an adult for someone who's grown up.

Colouring your Day

Some people make strong and unchanging assumptions about things. They view life as clear blocks of immovable colour: 'This is black, this is red and this is blue – end of story!'

Others allow for shades of colour in life, aware there are many different tones within the colour red. Even black is a variety of shades before reaching grey.

And then there are those who allow not only for shade but also change. These people do not assume today's colour is necessarily yesterday's. If it is light blue today, it could be charcoal grey tomorrow and crimson red at a later date. Who knows? What was green at lunch could be yellow by tea.

How shall I colour my day?

The Old Cottage

The old cottage was dark now and the owner's funeral just a memory. Much had been cleared out, but the old lady's kettle still sat in the kitchen, along with her rusting scales; while her home-made curtains, once maroon, covered the windows in the front room. There was even some wood in the fireplace, cold and unused.

The young woman opened the old curtains. There was a fine view across the fields and she'd already decided on the colour for the bathroom. The new carpets would be arriving in a fortnight and she could be living here within a month or two.

Later, she was meeting the old lady's son, who lived nearby. It was a courtesy call really, for it was her house now. But he had wished it, and who knows? It might help them both.

Each and every day, we meet things dying and things newborn – and pay our respects to both.

The Drowning

'He fallen in! He fallen in!' the little boy screams, running to get his dad, wanting him to save the man, now deep under-water, plummeting downwards, and no one moving, no one caring.

'Man gonna die! Save man, Daddy!'

His dad is shocked by the tears. He's only been in the kitchen five seconds, having left his son watching sport on TV.

'A perfect dive!' declares the commentator excitedly.

As we go about our daily business, it's not that we don't see things clearly, it's just that we only see the half of them.

The Clown's Apprentice

The boy was getting irritable and beginning to sulk; this was much harder work than expected.

'What's your problem?' asked the clown.

'Isn't it time for a break?'

'A break? You'll have a break when you've mastered the skills.'

This was not what the boy had anticipated when he'd signed up to be the clown's apprentice. He'd thought that clowning around was just that – clowning around, just another fun fad to dabble in. He hadn't realized there were skills to be mastered, a discipline to be learned. He felt like giving up.

'Everything is work,' said the clown as they sat exhausted with some circus coffee and a doughnut. 'Every pie in the face, every knockdown, every foot in the wet paint, every chase – these things are work: focused energy. You get nowhere and understand nothing without work, my friend. Happy work.'

8

The
Welcoming
Void

The Big Top at Midnight

It was an unusual circus act, not one anyone had seen before.

And no one saw it last night either, for it was midnight and the big top was empty when the clown stood alone in the ring, quite still in the dark sawdust space. Apart from his clown's hat, which he held in his hand, he was naked.

And this was not the first time; he'd entered this void before.

Because there were occasions, amid the make-up and applause, when he found it hard to remember who he was.

Beyond the Gates of Emptiness

Imagine walking through a big city, crowded with people, traffic and buildings; full of chatter, rush and hard shapes. Walk on – it takes a while – until you reach the gates of emptiness, and then, if you dare, go through.

Once inside, it may take some getting used to, for here is a different place, with neither talky-talk nor colourful form. Instead, you find silence, where the mind can be emptied of its favourite illusions.

People think form – the chattering, hard-edged world we know so well – is reality. But these things are only representations of truth, for before some thing is no thing.

Here beyond the gates of emptiness a building cannot exist; it would first have to dismantle itself. Neither can belief or social structures exist; they would first need to melt. Nor can rush exist; restlessness dissipates in the endless air of eternity.

But you can exist here, so don't rush away. Before form, you were no form. You are getting back to your roots.

Going Bowling

I have a bowl.

It's turquoise blue in colour; simple painted pottery from the Greek island of Rhodes.

It's too small to be a fruit bowl, too large to be a cereal or dessert bowl, and it sits rough and sparse on my table.

I am fond of this bowl. I'd contemplated it in the shop throughout my stay, wondering whether it was for me. Only on the final day came the decision to buy.

But I haven't told you the most important aspect of this bowl, and it is this: it is empty. Always has been, always will be. I have no wish for it to hold anything. Instead, I wish it to hold nothing and thereby guard the precious gift of space in me.

I hold it when I am busy inside with darting thoughts or emotional swirl and I am grateful for its emptying, clarifying force.

When finally I feel nothing, I put it down. Perhaps now I am ready for something.

I like bowling.

Harmony

'Harmony – that was it! That was what came out of the silence – a gentle rhythm, the strain of a perfect chord, the music of the spheres, perhaps.

It was enough to catch that rhythm, momentarily to be myself a part of it. In that instant I could feel no doubt of man's oneness with the universe … the universe was a cosmos, not a chaos; man was as rightfully a part of that cosmos as were the day and night.'

These were the reflections of the pioneering Admiral Byrd, the American polar explorer and aviator, in 1934, when he was alone for five months at a weather base in the Antarctic.

Here, in this bleak void, he experienced two common mystical experiences: a deep sense of unity with nature and the universe, allied to feelings of great peace and tranquillity.

Critics would say this was just the sad delusion of a lonely man in a frozen waste. Freud thought so, calling such experiences 'regression', the return of the adult to the mother's breast, where oneness with the world was all the child knew.

Maybe theirs is the deeper wisdom, however; maybe to be childlike is awareness enhanced, not diminished. As Jesus said to the shocked adults of his day, 'Unless you become as children…'

The child is happy to be one with all things, including the void.

Clouding the Issue

I'm contemplating the clouds today and floating some cotton-wool thoughts.

For good or ill, clouds do give the sky much of its character. Like our emotions, they are changing and ever variable, adjusting in colour and type.

Clouds can look solid and opaque, and on dark days prove a heavy and dominating presence across the landscape. Though apparently they are 99 per cent empty and not solid at all. The appearance of solidity is a trick of reflected light on the water droplets.

There's not much we can do about the sky, of course. Sometimes it's blue and sometimes it isn't.

And things do change, as we know. Often the warmth of the sun dissolves the moisture of the clouds.

It's good that our soul sky is blue, though clouds do pass through.

Love Is Not All You Need

In the thirteenth century, a German mystic called Meister Eckhart took something of a risk. He told people there was something more important than love.

'What could that be?' everyone asked. 'Isn't love meant to be the best thing ever?'

Not according to Eckhart – he put detachment ahead of love.

At first sight, it seems ridiculous. After all, I don't see Hollywood posters advertising: 'One of the greatest detachment stories ever!'

Neither do I hear a lot of 'detachment' songs on my radio.

But Eckhart was insistent. He said that until we learned detachment, our love was more about ourselves than anyone else; that until we detached ourselves from the tyranny of roller-coaster emotions and frenetic thoughts, there was no true self to offer anyone else.

Detach yourself from these outer senses, he said, *and you become aware of your inner place, the naked flame of intent flickering in the stillness.*

The Small Shop Debate

It's hard to tell with small shops, isn't it? I mean, some are just small, end of story – what you see is what you get. If something isn't on display, it probably isn't there. Availability is limited; best try somewhere else if you can't find what you're looking for.

But with other small shops, appearance deceives. Perhaps their owners have extended out the back or dug a cellar below, where further goods can be stored. It's still a small shop and not everything can be displayed, but that doesn't mean something isn't there.

In ourselves, we too are looking to increase space and the possibility of understanding. We too are looking to dismantle the tight and cramped psychological structures that so constrain us and create something more spacious within.

It's true that all small shops are small, but true also that some are surprisingly big.

The Truth Mirror Comes Up with Nothing

Truth Mirror: Well, you'll have to let go of them.

Seeker: I can't let go of them!

TM: They're not helping.

S: *Not helping?!* They're holding me together!

TM: Your certainties do not hold you together and I've got a better idea.

S: What – I let go of *my* certainties, and adopt *yours* instead?!

TM: No one is helped by other people's certainties and I'm not offering you mine.

S: Good.

TM: Second-hand experiences are like second-hand shoes – they don't fit happily.

S: So if I'm not adopting your creed, what am I adopting?

TM: Nothing really.

S: Oh, that's helpful! Glad I'm not paying for this.

TM: You're paying for it every second while you cling to your old formulations.

S: Is that so? Yet all you offer instead is 'nothing really'!

TM: Have you ever contemplated the winter soil?

S: Not often.

TM: That's because it's nothing really.

S: Precisely.

TM: But consider what emerges come the spring…

The Wider Path

You make time for inaction each day, to protect your actions from being mad.

You remove your watch, turn the clock face away and escape for a moment the slavery of time.

You remove your shoes, because you don't need to be anywhere or rush to anyone's aid.

The phone is off, because if people are worth your attention, they're also worth your withdrawal.

You sit or kneel, comfortable yet alert, for you wish neither to fidget nor to fall asleep.

Your palms are upwards, for you are daring to be open as you review the last 24 hours. Mindful of events and feelings, you allow all things into view without judgement.

And so it is you become a wider path for reality to run through, first in the stillness and then beyond.

Naked Intent

Naked intent is you sitting in the rain. Lightning flashes and wind lashes your face as you shout your wishes and deepest desires into the squall.

Not that the words are important, for you are beyond words now, and way beyond thoughts, as you pierce the dark clouds of unknowing above you with sharp darts of longing love. And you scream until you can scream no more.

Enough! Both your lungs and heart are spent.

And later, as you wander home in the stilling storm, you have to wonder: 'Just what have I done?'

You're not sure. But you do know that you longed for something and expressed that longing so intently that just for a moment, nothing else mattered.

Naked intent.

A Wise Person at Work

This is the story of a wise person. It concerns a mad professor.

The mad professor was really very untidy and messy. He was brilliant, of course, but could get lost in his own study, such was the chaos.

Fortunately he had a cleaner who came in once a week and sorted things out. She couldn't do his brilliant work for him, but how he loved the clear space that was left by her visits.

Sometimes he was so happy he even danced around the lamp in the corner before returning to work!

And this is what wise people like the cleaner do – they create space, inner or outer, in which others can live and work more happily.

Particle Physics on the Train

I try and notice something new every day, because new things are very polite. They wait to be asked before making an appearance.

Today, as I am reading a journal left on the train, my eyebrows are raised in surprise. As the train passes through fields and farmsteads, I am reading about particle physics and discovering that when viewed with extreme magnification, matter shows itself to be made up mostly of space. This is true even of bricks and iron girders, which have always seemed quite solid to me.

I have been mistaken, however. When a brick is placed under the magnifying glass, solidity and permanence are revealed to be illusions and spacious fluidity is confirmed.

I am so engrossed in all this that I miss the coffee trolley passing through. I am irritated, but then allow my initial reaction to become less solid. As with bricks, there is a surprising amount of space in our emotions; they are much less solid than we imagine.

I leave the journal on the train, as someone left it for me. Others may need to know about our spacious universe.

Talking to David

I was talking to David in Florence.

David was Michelangelo's statue of the Jewish boy hero, standing over seven feet tall in the Accademia di Belle Arti. As Vasari said, 'Whoever has seen this work need not trouble to see another work executed in sculpture.'

I was asking David if there was a moment when he knew how wonderfully he would turn out. He was once a block of stone, of course, and the apple of no one's eye. Yet in the hands of his creator, he became something entirely different. So was there an 'Aha!' moment when he realized how fine he would be?

David thought a while and then shook his fine head.

'You must remember,' he said, 'that sculpting is a precarious business. You can never be quite sure how things are working out and in the early days, I had no idea what I'd be. Simply no idea at all! How could I have? I was just a block of stone! Towards the end, I was more conscious of the gentle and patient chisel work as I felt myself emerging and then it was a mix of fear and awe, I think. But there was not one moment, but many moments.'

Making It Rhyme

The poet is having a hard time of it,
trying to get her work to rhyme.
Not usually a problem for her;
things flow effortlessly as a rule.
But there are no rhymes today and here's why:

She's attempting to put the truth of her life into verse.
Yet the more she reflects,
the more her truth doesn't really rhyme at all,
and can't quite be organized like that.

'Please give us more of your lovely rhymes!' say the people.
'I'm not sure I can today,' says the poet.
'Oh, go on!' they say. 'We find them so reassuring. They box
things up so cleverly and so well!'
'Yes,' says the poet. 'I think that's the problem.'

If the truth won't rhyme, do you go for the rhyme or the truth?

Courage beneath the Surface

I contemplate the flower. Yet more than delighting in its beauty this morning, I find myself admiring its courage. Truly, here is a story of courage beyond the call of duty.

I remember it when it was a seed, you see – a rather hard and self-contained little object. In that state there was nothing to link it with the colourful glory I now view. It stayed hidden in a seed packet at the back of my drawer for years, showing no signs of anything. And if I hadn't come across it when looking for some matches, it would have stayed there a good deal longer.

But here's the thing: once taken from the packet and put in the soil, it chose its own death. It allowed the soil to dismantle its boundaried little existence. It meant the end of everything it knew of itself, a terrible void of change and struggle.

Such courage and, I have to say, such trust.

Getting Wise

If wisdom could be acquired through information, there'd be no shortage of wise people on this planet. With the information highway at our internet fingertips, there'd be sages everywhere and a 'wise consultancy centre' on every street corner. No generation has had even a hundredth of the information we can lay our hands on in an instant.

Only it hasn't made us wise – not in the least. Some would say it has made us more stupid, promoting the impression of wisdom without the substance. We're ever hopeful and keep convincing ourselves that if we just buy the right book, we'll find a short cut. But there are no short cuts, for as the Mad Hatter reminded us in *Alice in Wonderland*, 'How you get there is where you'll arrive.' Attempt a short cut to wisdom and you'll find yourself short-changed.

How is wisdom acquired? Not through information, but through your state of being; wisdom is state-dependent. As Maurice Nicol said, 'As one's level of being increases, receptivity to higher meaning increases. As one's being decreases, the old meanings return.'

When you're tired of old meanings, consider the state you're in.

Understanding the Time

Socrates went to his imprisonment and death with some willingness. He could have escaped from Athens; there was opportunity. But after years of soldiering and keen debate, he seemed more inclined to accept things as they were, which led to his death from hemlock poisoning.

The last days of Jesus were not dissimilar. After three years of intense action and confrontation with the religious authorities, he became passive after his garden arrest by the military. He took no one on, refusing to plead on his own behalf. Instead, he accepted the savage outcome.

When Agrippinus was told that the Roman Senate had begun a trial against him, with the possibility of either death or exile, he continued his daily routine. When a messenger bought the news that he had been condemned, he calmly asked if he was to be put to death or banished. When told it was banishment, he began to make arrangements for moving.

There's a time for everything – a time for striving and a time for acceptance.

An Ending to Die for

When visiting the bereaved, I was often surprised by how surprised they were. Take Elizabeth, for instance. Her husband Bert may have been 87 and a lifelong smoker with lungs like tar buckets, but his death was a complete shock! 'How could this be?!' she asked angrily.

Human beings die all the time, of course, young and old. But Bert? Why him? Elizabeth really couldn't understand that. It was as if she had made him a separate being, one more important than others.

Once, when visiting an undertaker, I was able to lie in an empty coffin. Wonderful! The wooden sides pressed against me, but a sense of life spilled out.

As the former slave and Stoic philosopher Epictetus said, 'Let death and exile and every other thing that appears dreadful be daily before our eyes, but most of all death, and you will never think of anything mean, nor will you desire anything extravagantly.'

Let us not be surprised by death but make friends with it. And sooner rather than later.

The Welcoming Void

The darkness is total. Blacker than magic, more brilliant than light, it is a vast outbreak of nothing, unfenced by horizon. Here is deep space: luminous, shiny as hot tar, oozing existence – like a black cat stretching out in the bright sun.

Here is a velvet pool of emptiness, a liquid vacuum of pure possibility. It is absolute nothing, full only of absence and unmade creation. Here is the hollow place, the holy place, beyond all things physical and knowable.

North of north, south of south and east of eternity, here is nothing. And how nothing gives birth to something is a great wonder. Nothing into something, something from nothing, as from this dark barn of spontaneity and peace, all phenomena emerge; as from this womb of zero, stories arise like a butterfly breaking clear and fluttering free, so fragile, beautiful and brief.

Have a good day.

When the Ferryman Comes

When death arrives to collect me and my baggage, I will not jump to attention or act in haste from some half-remembered sense of duty; neither will I leap into his car in fluster, panic or dread.

Rather, I will ask for a few moments to sit with everything, for I have a story to tell; a story of what I did and when, and why.

So, while death waits, like a ferryman on a tea break, I gather together the community of voices who have lived my life – gather them together and say thank you. Yes, thank you! Oh – and we all agree that we did our best and that no one need feel ashamed, absolutely no one.

We did our best, half-knowing but wholehearted, and now it's time to go.

9
The Final Surrender

The Border Guards

If you ever attempt to question your bankrupt personality, you will find yourself roughly turned away by the border guards. They have been posted there to ensure you don't trespass on forbidden territory or ask awkward questions. If you did, you might see through to your true self.

No one knows how long the guards have been there or quite when they started their watch. To be honest, they don't even know themselves! They've been on guard so long they've lost all sense of time and quite forgotten why they are there.

'Why are we here?' asks one of them, with a cobweb hanging from his nose. 'I mean, what exactly are we guarding?'

'I don't know,' says the other, covered in the dust of time.

'Well, if you don't know, I certainly don't!'

'Given the time we've been here, though, you'd imagine it'd be important.'

'Maybe. Do your legs ache?'

'Terribly, yes – really badly.'

To discover who you are, you will need to question what you've become. It's time to speak with the guards and politely suggest much-needed retirement.

The Bonfire

Have you ever built a bonfire?

I love bonfires – warming and consuming, bright and destroying, wonderful and frightening. They've had different roles down the years. In the past, they were sometimes beacons on the coast, warning ships away from rocks. At other times, they were a celebration, lit to announce national success. These days, often as not, they are simply built at the bottom of the garden for the purpose of clearance, or roasting chestnuts.

But whatever the blaze, the glory of the fire is ultimately the glory of surrender. The wood surrenders to the flame and becomes something quite different. Before, it was cold logs and boxes piled on top of each other. Now? Well, it's something else entirely, quite unrecognizable, like the person whose life is somehow shot through with the flame of another life – a life of wonder, courage, compassion and warmth.

Surrender isn't the fashion, of course. Surrender is for losers, according to some. But try telling that to the bonfire or the candle. They know surrender makes them what they are, when they surrender to the flame.

Oh, and don't worry – nothing of true worth is ever destroyed in the blaze – only the dross.

Your goodness is wonderfully flame-resistant.

When We Haven't a Prayer

Some people say we simply haven't a prayer, but I don't find this to be true.

We can't always manage a prayer ourselves, of course. Perhaps we try, but it feels dry and manufactured, a cheap tin cymbal of a sound when we wished for a full orchestra. Or maybe the whole business of prayer feels mad, ridiculous and pathetic – a childish nonsense and not for us. We haven't a prayer and we don't want one, thank you very much!

And so the day prays for us, echoing through our body holy lines from another place. Perhaps it's the blessing of the ticket man's smile at the station, unbidden but bright; or an aroma on the street, or in a bakery or paint shop, taking you back across the years in sacred recollection. Or is it the scraped shoes of the beggar by the cashpoint, making you sad; or the brick tunnel into which the dark-watered canal disappears, all mystery and unknown...?

When we don't have a prayer, the universe is kind, scooping us up into one larger and more compelling. A full orchestra, in fact.

A Table the Size of the World

I like the simple writing of Thich Nhat Hanh, particularly when he asks me to consider a table.

A table exists because of things that we might regard as quite unconnected to tables – things from a non-table world. There's the forest, for instance, where the wood grew and was cut; the sun and rain, year after year, which made the wood possible; the carpenter who cut the wood, and the carpenter's ancestors and parents. And then there's the iron ore that became the nails and the screws; those who worked in the factory where the nails were made; the families and businesses who benefited from the wages earned there.

These are all things from the non-table world, yet crucial to the table's existence. If you took away any of these elements and returned them to their source – the nails to iron ore, the wood to the forest, the carpenter to the womb – then the table would no longer exist.

A person who can look at a table and see the universe, says Thich Nhat Hanh, that person is on the way.

Spirituality? It's the art of making connections.

The Soldier in the Middle

Battles are more clearly seen from the hill
than on the ground;
and for the troops in the ranks, it's hard to
know anything.

So the soldier in the middle can't be sure.
Those up ahead, at the front,
speak of a great victory coming.
While those behind, reporting from the back,
speak of crushing defeat.

But the soldier in the middle,
who can see neither front nor back,
can't be sure.
He can speak of what he knows,
but not of what he doesn't know.

So instead he looks after the ladybird
that crawls up his arm –

And wonders how the daisies grew overnight.

A Hell of a Day

When Billy died and was unjustly sent to hell, several local residents signed a petition for his release. They delivered the document to the appropriate authorities, but it had no effect. So they hurried home. Apart from anything else, it was very hot down there.

But with an election approaching, the local MP also took up the cause.

'I think you should let him out!' he shouted through a megaphone, whilst standing as near as he could get to the gates. But no one seemed to take any notice, so he too hurried home. Apart from anything else, it was very hot down there.

So Billy's dad decided to sort it out himself. He didn't sign anything or shout through a megaphone. He just burnt his hands opening the gates, scalded his face stepping inside and sweated blood carrying young Billy out and then home.

Love enters the hell of others, as opposed to posturing on the sidelines.

When the Ego Sings

As Herman Hesse observed in his short novel *Siddartha*, we can have too much knowledge, too many precious sacred verses, too many ritual rules and too much spiritual industry.

We can be so busy staying a step ahead of everyone, so bent on being spiritual, wise and high-minded, that our ego dances in unfettered delight.

'Watch them make a god out of the *process* of spirituality and not the *fruit!*' sings the ego. 'Hah! More, more!'

For Hesse, it was not about the game of spirituality, but the experience. As he wrote: 'The only thing of importance to me is being able to love the world, without looking down on it, without hating it and myself – being able to regard it and myself and all beings with love, admiration and reverence.'

The ego's not singing now.

Beginnings and Endings

There is a simple meditation that takes you around the world in less than 80 days. In fact, you'll be back within a few minutes and can wear slippers throughout.

Some call it 'The points of the compass' meditation, others 'The meditation of universal benevolence'. However, naming it is less important than doing it.

So, having got your bearings, stand, sit or kneel and face north.

Think with love and tenderness of all those you know who live north of you.

Enter into their joys and sorrows as you are able and let the hand of your affection and blessing rest upon their heads.

Then think of those unknown to you who live to the north of you. Exercise love and compassion towards them, as you are able. There might be a news story in your head to help you, but whatever you may or may not know, this is mainly about attitude and spirit.

Then turn to the east and then south and then west and do likewise.

Finally, hold the world inside you, like a seed sown deep in the soil, and be on your sweet way.

The Flame-Keeper

In the old days, the flame-keeper was an important figure in the village. He protected the precious flame that warmed and lit the people's vulnerable lives.

The calling was for all seasons. Amid high winds, lashing rain, deep darkness and frosty cold, the flame-keeper nurtured the orange embers. How else would anyone survive? If the fire died – well, it didn't bear thinking about.

In similar fashion, through fair and foul, the mystic kindles the flame within, stirring the embers of courage, kindness, clarity, simplicity, reverence, openness, union and hope.

In the hearth of the heart, the flickering flame is fed.

And That Will Be Fine

The old man does what he can do. He potters in the garden, slowly achieving small but useful things.

Once he did more. When physically able, he created things and received applause in the world. But those days are gone and now he does what he can, clearing the leaves, feeding fish in the pond, going about his tasks.

One day, even these things will pass. And then he'll lie still, weak throughout, and take visitors and small sips of tea.

And that will be fine. Because we do what we can; this is the truth. As the days become weeks and the months become years, we do what we can until it's given us to do more or do less.

And whichever it is, that will be fine.

The Long Journey Home

His job involved long car journeys up and down the land.

He remembers particularly the winter nights – weary eyes peering into the darkness ahead and the strong desire to be home.

He remembers counting away the minutes and hours, enclosed in his metal shell, frustrated by hold-ups, low on petrol and feeling the rage of the roads. Life could be better.

But once, and it happened quite unbidden, he heard the whisper of a cathedral choir. On the fast-fizzing motorway, there on the radio were sound and song from another world. And as he listened, the metal shell melted. He was no longer trapped, but one with the night.

And strange, most strange – he said he felt he was home. Right there, right then on the road, the music somehow took him home, though with many miles to go.

The Mystic's Bench

There is a bench inside us. Were you aware of this? It doesn't show on X-rays apparently, but then neither does kindness, so what have we learned?

This bench is wonderfully positioned at the edge of three lands: our inner world, the world outside us and the world beyond us.

From this vantage point, there are extensive views of all three realities; clear and compassionate seeing in every direction, when the skies are haze-free. On a clear day, you can see great distances.

Some call it 'The Mystic's Bench'. Others call it 'The Bench of the Three Worlds'.

As you can imagine, this seat is a fine and exhilarating place to go, though the rumours are true — it is not always comfortable.

A Brilliant Day

I don't know what a good day is for you.
How could I? We are different.
Your nightmare is my dream and vice versa.

But here's a good day for us all:
it's a very good day when you visit your own
malice, spite and judgement factory
eager for fresh supplies –
and find the shelves empty!
When you visit this sad factory and find
the machinery defunct,
the offices closed,
and the workforce gone,
laid off due to lack of business.

'The order books have been empty too long,'
says the foreman locking the gates.

What a brilliant day!

Father to Daughter

It was father to daughter, on the day she left home.

'All packed?'

'All packed.'

'It looks a bit bare!'

'It does, doesn't it?'

They were standing together in her empty room, a room cleared of her things. Soon the removals crew would be along for the final action and there were tears in both their eyes. It was time to go, yes; yet so much was ending.

'So now you must go and change the world!' said the father.

She smiled, because she wished to; she wished so much to change the world.

'Remembering always—'

'Remembering what?' she asked.

'Remembering always to love yourself and the world exactly as they are.'

On a Level

Here's a fact not much discussed. You cannot judge someone and know them. If you are judging them, they must remain an eternal stranger to you.

This is why our categories of 'right' and 'wrong' are so unhelpful. They cut us off from people, which is the root of hell on Earth, separation instead of union.

In India, during the first half of the twentieth century, Mahatma Gandhi was a man caught between three determined and separate power blocks – Hindu, Muslim and British. All reviled him in turn, imagining he was on the side of the other(s). But amidst it all, and through endless meeting and negotiation, Gandhi referred to all opponents as 'my friend', because for him, this was the bigger truth. There was no one to judge, just something to create.

So we will put down judgement today. We will resist the rush to the moral high ground and stay on a level with people –

and perhaps see someone for the first time.

The Frog and the Fly

The frog sits in the puddle,
marvelling at the vast expanse of water before him;
quite unaware of the oceans beyond.

And the fly whose lifespan is the summer,
knows nothing of the winter snows.

We see life from our small perspective,
and make too much of pointless things.
Daily we allow them to insert worry and unrest in our lives.

Beyond our small-world distinctions between success and
failure,
happy and sad, rich and poor, right and wrong, useful and
useless –
beyond these things lies the whole, the whole that holds all
parts.

Journey to this place;
be neither the frog nor the fly.
Avoid distraction,
and travel from part to whole.

It is a different land – as different as a puddle and an ocean.

Trusting the Day

I will trust this day.
I will trust what happens and the way it works out.
I will trust it comes to bless,
and has no intention other than to hold me in its loving arms.

When I lose this trust, my behaviour becomes most odd.
I attempt to control situations and people,
or run around like a chicken in a panic.
Perhaps I fill my head with noise,
or my life with activity.
I may start the blame game, with myself or others,
become smug on my imaginary moral high ground,
or perhaps declare in loud despair: 'It's all going wrong – just
like it always does!'

As I say, when I lose a sense of trust, my behaviour becomes
most odd.

So I will trust today and all it brings.
For when it is so, and the trust is strong,
all is quite perfect
and all is quite well.

A Strange Masterpiece

A Zen painting kit is unlike other painting kits, though it may not be to everyone's taste.

It all starts normally enough. You take your brush, dip it into water and then paint an image on the board provided. Your creation is there before your eyes, as clear as day, but not for long – for the image fades as the board dries. So you then reflect a while, dip the brush in water again, paint something else – and watch as that too disappears from view.

This might feel frustrating, but there is a reason behind it. The impermanence of the image you create deepens your appreciation and understanding of the impermanent nature of all things. Whether you perceive your painting as good or bad is of no consequence; neither does it matter whether it is a disturbing image or a pleasant one. You merely breathe it away as the image fades.

It's a masterpiece of letting go, of surrendering to the great flow.

Terry the Tree

Terry the tree was enjoying being a tree in the forest until one day the forester came along and asked if he minded being cut down for his own good. Mind? Terry certainly minded! But because he trusted the forester, who was his dearest friend, he said, 'OK, go ahead.' So Terry was cut down and sent crashing to the ground.

The next day Terry was lying there, looking up at the sky, when the forester came along and asked if he minded being sliced in half and then scraped out inside. Mind? Terry minded a great deal! But because he trusted the forester, who was his dearest friend, he said, 'OK, go ahead.'

So Terry was sliced in half and scraped out, after which he was carried many miles to a dry land. He was then placed by a river and became a channel for the water to flow from there to the parched earth all around. What wonderful crops were soon growing! And how Terry laughed in delight!

Things happen to me — victim; things happen with me — activist; things happen through me — spiritual being.

Golden Thoughts

The twentieth-century monk and author Thomas Merton did much to bring the spiritualities of East and West together and talked of a small kernel of gold that is the essence of each of us.

It's a wonderful image, a picture of the essential you – there, at the core of your being, a kernel of gold, a golden glow of intense value, quite unsullied by fear, bitterness or rage.

However, though closer than close, it may be a journey to find that kernel, to sense its inner reality. There's a lot of lost treasure in the world, and your essence may be some of it.

Real freedom is to come and go from that centre as the day allows and demands, and to be quite able to forego anything that is not directly related to it.

Dross can shine for a time but should not be mistaken for gold.

From Now On

May now the armies within, which struggle,
begin to make peace,
face the fears which so fill, which cripple and kill,
make them foolish.
May anxiety know, it's the end of the show.
It is over.
May the longings which ask, which knock, now bask
in God's smile.
May life's limits which stress, frustrate and depress,
hear an answer.
And may your name on God's heart, be the start,
of all ventures ahead.

Notes

Notes

Notes

Notes

Notes

Notes

Notes

Notes

Hay House Titles of Related Interest

Fuck It,
by John Parkin

Guardians of Being,
by Eckhart Tolle

Inspiration,
by Dr Wayne W. Dyer

You Can Have What You Want,
by Michael Neill

You Can Heal Your Life,
by Louise L. Hay

JOIN THE HAY HOUSE FAMILY

As the leading self-help, mind, body and spirit publisher in the UK, we'd like to welcome you to our family so that you can enjoy all the benefits our website has to offer.

 EXTRACTS from a selection of your favourite author titles

 COMPETITIONS, PRIZES & SPECIAL OFFERS Win extracts, money off, downloads and so much more

 LISTEN to a range of radio interviews and our latest audio publications

 CELEBRATE YOUR BIRTHDAY An inspiring gift will be sent your way

 LATEST NEWS Keep up with the latest news from and about our authors

 ATTEND OUR AUTHOR EVENTS Be the first to hear about our author events

 iPHONE APPS Download your favourite app for your iPhone

 HAY HOUSE INFORMATION Ask us anything, all enquiries answered

join us online at **www.hayhouse.co.uk**

292B Kensal Road, London W10 5BE
T: 020 8962 1230 E: info@hayhouse.co.uk

We hope you enjoyed this Hay House book.
If you would like to receive a free catalogue featuring additional
Hay House books and products, or if you would like information
about the Hay Foundation, please contact:

Hay House UK Ltd
292B Kensal Road • London W10 5BE
Tel: (44) 20 8962 1230; Fax: (44) 20 8962 1239
www.hayhouse.co.uk

***

Published and distributed in the United States of America by:
Hay House, Inc. • PO Box 5100 • Carlsbad, CA 92018-5100
Tel: (1) 760 431 7695 or (1) 800 654 5126;
Fax: (1) 760 431 6948 or (1) 800 650 5115
www.hayhouse.com

***

Published and distributed in Australia by:
Hay House Australia Ltd • 18/36 Ralph Street • Alexandria, NSW 2015
Tel: (61) 2 9669 4299, Fax: (61) 2 9669 4144
www.hayhouse.com.au

***

Published and distributed in the Republic of South Africa by:
Hay House SA (Pty) Ltd • PO Box 990 • Witkoppen 2068
Tel/Fax: (27) 11 467 8904
www.hayhouse.co.za

***

Published and distributed in India by:
Hay House Publishers India • Muskaan Complex • Plot No.3
B-2• Vasant Kunj • New Delhi - 110 070
Tel: (91) 11 41761620; Fax: (91) 11 41761630
www.hayhouse.co.in

***

Distributed in Canada by:
Raincoast • 9050 Shaughnessy St • Vancouver, BC V6P 6E5
Tel: (1) 604 323 7100
Fax: (1) 604 323 2600

***

Sign up via the Hay House UK website to receive the Hay House
online newsletter and stay informed about what's going on with your
favourite authors. You'll receive bimonthly announcements
about discounts and offers, special events, product highlights,
free excerpts, giveaways, and more!
www.hayhouse.co.uk